My Big Book of WILD Animals

What's Going On?

A four-mile patch of rain forest usually contains up to 125 different species of mammals, 400 kinds of birds, 100 reptiles, 60 amphibians, and countless insect species. But each day, about 74,000 acres of the earth's rain forests are destroyed, threatening the animals and plants that live there.

In North America the habitat for wildlife is also disappearing. Eighty years ago, mountain lions were plentiful but are now threatened. Grizzly bears, which once roamed the west in great numbers, have dwindled to fewer than 1,000 in the lower 48 states. Wetlands, which are home to many bird, reptile, and amphibian species, are shrinking and becoming polluted.

The large mammals of Africa may be gone in 20 years. African elephants are still hunted for their tusks, and their habitat is being eliminated. Ninety percent of the black rhinos are gone, and gorillas are losing their habitat.

It's Up to Us to Change Things

The impact that humans have had on the habitats and wildlife has been destructive because our choices have been destructive. If we change our attitude and our choices, we can make a difference. And that means that every single person—no matter where you live, no matter how old you are—can be part of the solution.

My Big Book of WILD Animals

Produced in Partnership
with the SAN DIEGO
ZOO.

ideals children's books.
Nashville, Tennessee

ISBN-13: 978-0-8249-5543-4

Published by Ideals Children's Books
An imprint of Ideals Publications
A Guideposts Company
535 Metroplex Drive, Suite 250
Nashville, Tennessee 37211
www.idealsbooks.com

Prepress by Precision Color Graphics, Franklin, Wisconsin

Printed and bound in Mexico by RR Donnelley

Library of Congress Cataloging-in-Publication Data

My big book of wild animals / produced in partnership with the San Diego Zoo .
   p. cm.
  Includes index.
  ISBN-13: 978-0-8249-5543-4 (alk. paper)
  ISBN-10: 0-8249-5543-9 (alk. paper)
  1. Animals—Juvenile literature. I. San Diego Zoo.
  QL49.M888 2007
  590—dc22
               2007005344

10 9 8 7 6 5 4 3 2 1

All photographs, unless otherwise noted, are provided by Creative Services, Zoological Society of San Diego.

Spot illustrations by Mike Dammer
Design by Eve DeGrie

Ideals Publications is a proud supporter of the San Diego Zoo and the San Diego Zoo's Wild Animal Park and will contribute 7% of the proceeds of each purchase of this item to support global conservation programs. The Zoological Society of San Diego is a California not-for-profit corporation located at 2920 Zoo Drive, San Diego, CA 92112. This purchase is not tax-deductible.

Wildbeasts™ is used by the San Diego Zoo® to promote worldwide conservation. Purchasing this product supports the San Diego Zoo's efforts to protect the survival of animals in captivity and those in the wild through research and education. The San Diego Zoo participates in international conservation projects in five geographical regions around the world.

We believe that even one endangered species is one too many. To learn more about Wildbeasts™, visit www.wildbeasts.org. To make a donation to the San Diego Zoo's conservation efforts, visit www.sandiegozoo.org.

Front cover photographs (clockwise): Sumatran Tiger, Eurasian Eagle-owl, Emerald Tree Boa, Giant Panda, Gorilla

Back cover photographs: Red-eyed Tree Frog, North Chinese Leopard

Page 1 photograph: Sumatran Tigers

CONTENTS

Three-horned Rhinoceros Beetle

Insects

WHAT IN THE WORLD ARE INSECTS?

- invertebrates (no backbone)
- exoskeletons
- have compound eyes
- have six legs
- have two antennae
- have a body divided into three parts: head, thorax, abdomen
- go through metamorphosis

INSECT STUFF

LONGEST: stick insect, 12 inches
HEAVIEST: Goliath beetle, 3.5 ounces
SMALLEST: tiny wasp, 0.08 inch
NUMBER OF SPECIES: nearly 1,000,000
CONSERVATION STATUS: many at critical risk, others threatened and vulnerable

TWO GROUPS OF INSECTS

Wingless insects: bristletails, silverfish

Winged insects: dragonflies, cockroaches, grasshoppers, stick insects, beetles, flies, butterflies, ants, and bees

Native Bee

Australian Walkingstick, Hatchling Nymph and Eggs

Spiny Stick Insect

Bee

European Honeybee on Fruit Tree Blossom

BURNING BEESWAX
Candles can be made from the wax in a honeycomb. These candles give off a honey-scented glow and burn cleanly and brightly.

Bee Laden with Pollen in Gazania

FLOWER POWER
All bees fly from flower to flower, sipping nectar and collecting grains of pollen. Flowers that attract bees are usually yellow, blue, and purple.

European Honeybee on Flower

WHERE IN THE WORLD ARE BEES?

RANGE: all continents except Antarctica

HABITAT: all habitats

SPINNING NECTAR INTO GOLD
Honeybees have a special tongue that sucks up sweet nectar. The bee stores it in a crop in its throat until it gets back to the hive. Here the nectar is turned into honey.

Bee Carrying Pollen to/from Aloes

IT TAKES A DOZEN
Bees gather nectar and pollen from flowers. It would take the nectar from 12 bees to make one teaspoon of honey.

Bees Swarming

Native Bee

DON'T BOTHER THE NATIVES
Native bees are bees that have always lived in an area and are able to survive without help from humans. These bees don't make honey or beeswax, but they pollinate many plants. They are called "super pollinators."

Native Bee

Rainbows of Bees
Bees may be black, brown, or banded with white, yellow, or orange stripes. All bees are covered with hair.

European Honeybee

MIRACLE OF THE HONEYCOMB

The honeycomb is made from beeswax secreted by glands on the worker bees' abdomens. The workers chew the wax and mold it into six-sided honeycomb cells that together form a sheet of honeycomb from two to four feet long. An empty honeycomb weighs just a few ounces, but when full of honey it can weigh many pounds.

Bee and White Floss Silk Tree Flower

Wanted: Worker Bee
The worker bees have many jobs:

- A newly hatched worker is the "cleaner."
- Days 3 to 10: Worker feeds the larvae and queen.
- Days 10 to 15: Worker builds the honeycomb.
- Day 16 to 20: Worker receives the pollen, stores it in the comb.
- Day 21 for a few days: Worker guards the hive.
- Finally, worker goes outside and gathers pollen.
- Worker bee dies.

QUEEN BEE

There is only one queen in each hive. The only thing the queen does is lay up to 2,000 eggs per day for as long as five years. The worker bees control how many eggs she lays with the amount of food they feed her.

THE DRONES

Drones are the few males in the hive. They spend their first days after hatching being fed by their sisters, then fly off to look for a queen. Drones have huge eyes to help them find a queen. Only the fastest drones catch the queens. After a drone catches a queen and mates, he dies.

WORKER BEES

Most of the bees in the hive are female worker bees. They build the honeycomb, care for the larvae, clean the hive, feed the queen, and collect the food. There are thousands of workers in a colony, sometimes up to 60,000 worker bees.

WHAT DID YOU SAY?

When a honeybee finds flowers with pollen, she brings a sample back to the hive. She shakes and wiggles her tail and spreads the flower scent to the others.

FRUIT GROWERS

We would not have some fruit if bees did not pollinate the flowers. These include almonds, apples, avocados, blueberries, cherries, cranberries, cucumbers, kiwis, melons, peaches, pears, plums, strawberries, and watermelons.

KILLER BEES

"Killer bees" are actually Africanized honeybees. They look like regular honeybees but are quick to defend their hive. They chase their enemies for longer distances and tend to gang up and sting. A single sting from one Africanized honeybee is no more dangerous than any other bee sting.

Bee with Bottlebrush

A TISKET, A TASKET, A HAIRY BEE BASKET

Hairs on the female bee's back legs form a sort of basket. When a bee visits a flower, she combs grains of pollen into her basket. Males do not collect pollen and don't have this "basket."

Busy as a Bee
Honeybees, bumblebees, and a few native bees live in hives. No honeybee or bumblebee can survive on its own.

THE BUZZ ON BEES

Native bees have the ability to buzz so hard that they cause flowers with tiny holes in them to release their pollen. Cultivated honeybees do not know how to "buzz pollinate."

PICK A FLAVOR

Honey has different flavors and colors, depending on which flowers the bees used to collect the nectar. Some of these are clover honey, orange-blossom honey, sourwood honey, and buckwheat honey.

Beetles

EYE SEE YOU

Most beetles have compound eyes that are divided into many six-sided compartments. Compound eyes are very sensitive to movement and can probably see in color.

BEETLE HOUSE

Most beetle species live on land. They tunnel underground, in wood, or in the carcasses of animals. Some beetles live in the nests of ants and termites.

I'd Rather Be Flying
Most beetles fly, although in a slow, clumsy manner.

Three-horned Rhinoceros Beetle

WHERE IN THE WORLD ARE BEETLES?

RANGE: almost everywhere except oceans, seas, and Antarctica

HABITAT: almost everywhere; most abundant in tropical rain forests

Rhinoceros Beetle

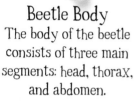

BEETLE HEAD
On the head are the beetle's eyes, mouth, brain, and antennae. Some horned beetles have extensions on their heads that look like horns or antlers.

ANTENNAE ALERT
Antennae on the beetle's head serve two functions. First, they are like feelers to help the beetle find food and, second, they alert the beetle to vibrations that could mean danger.

Beetle Body
The body of the beetle consists of three main segments: head, thorax, and abdomen.

Stag Beetle

BEETLE ABDOMEN

The abdomen contains the organs for digestion and reproduction. A tough exoskeleton and the wing cases (elytra) protect the beetle's soft membranes and keep the beetle from drying out or getting waterlogged.

BEETLE THORAX

Attached to the thorax are six legs and wings. Thick, hardened front wings cover most of the beetle's body and its back wings help protect the body.

Is That a Mouth?
Beetles' front jaws vary in size and shape. Beetles that eat nectar have tube-like mouths.

White-lined June Bug

Sunburst Diving Beetle Underwater

WHAT'S FOR DINNER?
Beetles eat almost everything: plants, other insects, carcasses, and dung. Some beetles live in water and eat fish and tadpoles. Many animals and even some carnivorous plants eat beetles.

BEETLE-MANIA
One-fourth of all animals on earth are beetles. They can be found almost everywhere, from deserts to lakes, rain forests to polar ice caps.

Sunburst Diving Beetle Swimming Underwater

FEELINGS, I GET FEELINGS
Tiny hairs on the beetles' bodies are called setae and allow the beetle to "feel" sound, smell, taste, and light.

Sunburst Diving Beetle Out of Water

BEETLE EGGS
Beetle eggs are soft and smooth and laid in soil, in wood, under tree bark, on leaves, or in carcasses. A female may lay several *thousand* eggs.

BEETLE GRUB
Beetle larvae hatch from eggs and look like worms or caterpillars. They have from one to six simple eyes and mouths for eating. They eat and grow, molting as they get bigger.

Grant's Rhinoceros Beetle in the Larva Stage

Metamorphosis
There are four stages in a beetle's life: egg, larva, pupa, adult.

DON'T EAT THE BEETLE
Leaf beetle larvae are so poisonous that Kalahari bushmen use them to tip their hunting arrows.

ARE THOSE LEGS I SEE?

Most beetles go through a pupal stage and develop legs, wings, and antennae. A few beetle families keep the features of the larva.

WHAT'S YOUR LEG STYLE?

All beetles have jointed legs. Ground beetles have long, slender legs and can move fast. Dung beetles have broad, ridged legs useful for digging. A water beetle's legs are curved and shaped like a paddle, helping them swim fast. Flea beetles have large hind legs for hopping.

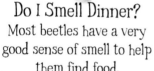

Do I Smell Dinner?
Most beetles have a very good sense of smell to help them find food.

White-lined June Bug

WING SPROUTS

When the adult beetle emerges from the pupal stage, its body is soft and pale. Soon, the body covering becomes hard and the beetle's true colors appear. The back wings and elytra push to the outside of the body.

Uh-Oh! I Can't Turn Over!
Most beetles have a hard time righting themselves when turned upside down.

Ladybug

BEETLES, BEETLES EVERYWHERE

Some common beetles are ladybugs, June bugs, weevils, lightning bugs or fireflies, borers, and potato bugs.

BEETLE PESTS

Many beetle species are pests and damage plants and transmit disease. Woodworm beetles eat furniture and wood floors; weevils attack crops, such as cotton, apples, and corn. The potato beetle can destroy a potato crop, but not all beetles are harmful. Farmers release ladybird beetles to eat aphids. Ground beetles feed on potato beetles.

Butterfly & Moth

Monarch Butterfly

SUPERSONIC BUTTERFLY

Most butterflies fly at five to 12 miles per hour. Skipper butterflies can fly at 37 miles per hour. A few butterflies fly as high as 10,000 feet. Some species can also cover long distances, like the monarch butterfly, which can migrate 2,000 miles or more.

Atlas Moth

A CHILD FOREVER!

Some Arctic moths spend 14 years as caterpillars.

Hecales Longwing Butterfly

WHERE IN THE WORLD ARE BUTTERFLIES & MOTHS?

RANGE: all continents except Antarctica

HABITAT: from tropical forests, to open grasslands, to Arctic tundra

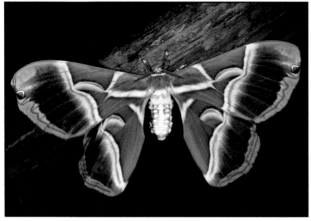

Cynthia Moth (or Silk Moth)

Hecales Longwing Butterfly

Butterfly or Moth?

Moths tend to have larger, fuzzier bodies than butterflies. Most moths fly at night, while most butterflies fly during the day. When resting, most moths flatten their wings on their bodies, while most butterflies hold them up against each other.

BUTTERFLY WINGS

The main structure of the wing is thin layers of chitin, a protein. These layers are so thin you can see through them. They are covered with tiny hairs which create the colors and patterns. The wings move in a figure eight motion that pushes the butterfly through the air.

Close-up of Blue Morpho Wing

Close-up of Tailed Jay Butterfly Wing

VAMPIRE MOTH

The Asian vampire moth lives up to its name. It has a tough nose to break through thick-skinned fruits, but sometimes it also sucks the blood of water buffalo or deer.

Look, Don't Touch!

Moth and butterfly wings are very delicate and can easily rip or tear from the slightest touch.

THE LIFE CYCLE OF A MOTH OR BUTTERFLY

1

EGG
An adult female lays her eggs on plants that the caterpillars can eat when they hatch. Some butterflies will lay their eggs on only one type of plant!

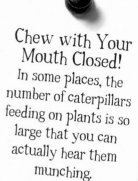

Chew with Your Mouth Closed!
In some places, the number of caterpillars feeding on plants is so large that you can actually hear them munching.

CATERPILLAR
When the caterpillar emerges, it eats the egg casing, then the plant. A caterpillar is a munching machine. It eats and grows. Each time the caterpillar gets too big for its skin, it sheds the skin.

2

METAMORPHOSIS
When it is time, the caterpillar sheds its skin for the last time and a hard casing forms, called a chrysalis or pupa. Moths add more protection; they spin a silky cocoon as well. Metamorphosis happens, and when the butterfly breaks out, it is an adult that can reproduce, fly in search of food, and migrate if necessary.

3

4

5

Monarch Butterfly

METAMORPHOSIS

Butterflies change from crawling caterpillars into winged beauties by a process called metamorphosis. When a caterpillar seals itself into a chrysalis, chemicals are released from its body that change and rearrange all the cells to create the butterfly's new shape, including its wings.

Tree Nymph Butterfly

Julia Butterfly

Tree Nymph Butterfly

Does It Taste Good to Your Feet?

Butterflies have taste sensors on their feet. By standing on a leaf, they can taste it to see if their caterpillars can eat it.

WHAT A LONG NOSE YOU HAVE

Most adult butterflies can't bite or chew. They eat mainly liquids like nectar, sap, and juices from fruits. Butterflies have a long, tubelike tongue called a proboscis, which works like a straw to suck up liquid. When butterflies are not using their tongue, it stays coiled up like a garden hose.

Giant Owl Butterfly

Julia Butterfly

Stick Insect

STICK INSECT STUFF

LENGTH: 1 to 12 inches

LIFE SPAN: 1 to 2 years

CONSERVATION STATUS: all vulnerable from human encroachment, pesticides, and habitat destruction

Vietnamese or Annam Walkingstick

NOW YOU SEE IT, NOW YOU DON'T

Some stick insect species have brightly colored wings that are invisible when folded against their body. When they feel threatened, they flash their wings, then immediately drop to the ground and hide their wings. The predator searches for a brightly colored insect but only sees a pile of drab, brown sticks on the ground!

Blowin' in the Wind

When stick insects need to move, they walk in a swaying motion, pretending to be a twig caught by the wind.

MASTERS OF DISGUISE

Stick insects have taken camouflage and imitation to the extreme by developing the appearance of a stick or twig. Typically these insects are shades of brown, although some may be green, black, gray, or blue. Most stick insect species are usually found sitting right out in the open within the leaves of a tropical tree.

FOOD CYCLE

Stick insects are herbivores that munch on leaves with their powerful jaws, called mandibles. Their droppings contain broken-down plant material that becomes food for other insects.

Vietnamese or Annam Walkingstick

BORN IN A GARBAGE DUMP

Some stick insects' eggs are covered with a hard shell that contains goodies that lure ants. The ants drag the egg into their nest and eat the shell. When the ants are full, they toss what's left, which includes the egg, into their nest garbage dump. The stick insect egg incubates, and a few months later the all-but-forgotten hatchling crawls out of the ant nest!

Spiny Stick Insect with Young and Eggs

WHERE IN THE WORLD ARE STICK INSECTS?

RANGE: all continents except Antarctica

HABITAT: tropical forests and woodlands

DROPS ALONG THE WAY

Some female stick insects drop one egg per day somewhere on the ground during their day's travels. The eggs are small and resemble seeds. By dispersing her eggs far and wide, the female prevents a predator from lunching on a cluster of her eggs.

What's a Leg or Two?
Juvenile walkingsticks can discard their legs to escape a predator's grasp. They will grow new legs at the next molt.

DINNER BY CANDLELIGHT

Even though stick insects avoid daytime predators, they are not safe from bats. The stick insect's elaborate camouflage doesn't help it in the dark. Bats that use echolocation hone in on the tiny noises made by stick insects and turn the insect into a tasty meal.

Thorny Stick Insect

A NYMPH'S LIFE

Stick insect hatchlings, called nymphs, hatch from the egg as miniature versions of adults. To reach adult size, the insect molts several times. Molting occurs when the exoskeleton is shed and the larger body that had grown inside it expands and hardens.

UNDER COVER OF DARKNESS

Stick insects are mostly nocturnal. They make a nutritious and filling meal for many birds, reptiles, spiders, and primates and, therefore, are safer under the cloak of darkness.

Giant Thorny Stick Insect

Baboon Spider

Spiders

WHAT IN THE WORLD ARE SPIDERS?

- invertebrates (no backbone)
- exoskeletons
- have eight legs
- have simple eyes
- have a body divided into two parts: cephalothorax and abdomen
- go through metamorphosis
- weave webs

Orb Weaver Spider

Tarantula

FOUR CLASSES OF SPIDERS

Tangle-web spiders. Messy looking, non-sticky webs found in bushes or buildings often called cobwebs. Spider hangs upside down in the middle of its web, waiting for ants or crickets to get tangled up. Black widow is a tangle-web spider.

Orb-web spiders. These spiders create the most familiar webs (think Halloween time!) made of a sticky silk to capture prey. It takes about 30 minutes to spin this type of web. Once prey is caught in the web, the spider quickly wraps it in more silk to keep it secure until dinnertime. Most spiders that spin orb-shaped webs build a new web every day, recycling their silk supply by eating the old web.

Funnel-web spiders. This group builds webs that funnel down into the entrance of their burrow. The spider waits inside the burrow for its next meal, such as a cockroach, to trip over one of the snaglines anchoring the web. The spider feels the vibration and dashes out to grab its prey. Sydney funnel web spider is a funnel-web spider.

Nursery-web spiders. Using their silk webbing for the egg sac, the female fastens the sac to some leaves and encloses it within a web to protect the eggs until they hatch.

Spiders

Fishing Spider

KISSIN' COUSINS?

Spiders are related to insects because they are both arthropods, but they are different in many ways. Spiders have two body parts, a cephalothorax and an abdomen, while insects have three. Spiders have eight legs while insects have six. In general, spiders possess simple eyes while many insects have compound eyes with much better vision.

WILL IT KILL ME?

All spiders are venomous, but only a small percentage are potentially dangerous to humans. Spiders use their venom to subdue their prey and only bite if cornered or trapped.

Black Widow

Chilean Rose Tarantula

JACK BE NIMBLE, JACK BE QUICK

The jumping spider can jump 40 times its own body length and leaps onto its prey. Thank goodness jumping spiders have excellent vision. Otherwise, they might miss and land who knows where!

OW, THAT HURTS!

Tarantulas flick special hairs—called urticating hairs—off their abdomens when disturbed. These hairs are barbed and lodge in the eyes and mucous membranes of would-be attackers.

WHERE IN THE WORLD ARE SPIDERS?

RANGE: all continents except Antarctica

HABITAT: all habitats

Can You Say AR-THRO-POD?
Arthropods are a group of animals with a segmented body, external skeleton, and jointed limbs.

Mexican Fireleg Tarantula

HOW MANY LEGS DOES IT TAKE?

Spiders are not insects. Spiders belong to a different group of animals called arachnida (arachnids). Arachnids have eight legs.

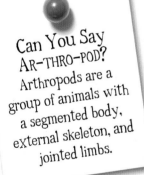

Green Lynx Spider

Orb Weaver Spider

SPIDER SILK?

Spider silk is the material that makes up a spider's web. It is the strongest known natural fiber in the world. Spider silk is used for crosshairs in guns, and the proteins in spider silk are being tested for use in bulletproof body armor. Spider silk, however, cannot be produced in large quantities, like that of the silk moth larvae.

Golden Spider

Spider Webs

A WEB IS WHAT YOU MAKE IT

Some spiders don't weave their own webs. They live as parasites on the webs of other spiders. One spider species builds a trapdoor in its web to ambush prey. Another spider species keeps a web handy to throw as a net over an unsuspecting fly!

Bird-eating Spider

YUM, YUM
Some people consider the Goliath bird-eating spider to be a tasty morsel when wrapped in a banana leaf and roasted over a fire.

AHOY! YOU SPIDERS
Fishing spiders are spiders that live *on* the water; they live their whole life floating. Diving bell spiders live *under* the water.

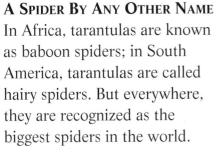

Minding Spider Business
Most tarantulas are busy minding their own business. If you don't bother them, they won't bother you. Honest!

A SPIDER BY ANY OTHER NAME
In Africa, tarantulas are known as baboon spiders; in South America, tarantulas are called hairy spiders. But everywhere, they are recognized as the biggest spiders in the world.

Fishing Spider

Tarantula

Mexican Fireleg Tarantula

HALF AND HALF
Like all spiders, tarantulas have two body segments: a cephalothorax and an abdomen. Plus they have strong jaws with venomous fangs.

New Clothes Diet
Adult tarantulas will stop feeding for several days to as long as several months before molting.

BACHELOR PADS
Some tarantulas dig a deep burrow and line it with silk webbing to keep sand and dirt from trickling in. Other tarantulas live on the ground under rocks, logs, or the shed bark of trees. Others live in webbed burrows in trees. These large spiders are solitary creatures, so there is only one spider per "house."

BORN TO SILK
The female weaves a silk cocoon in which to lay her eggs. After she lays from 75 to 1,000 eggs, she seals the cocoon with silk. The mom tarantula stands guard for six to nine weeks until her babies hatch. After two or three weeks, the babies go off on their own.

WHERE IN THE WORLD ARE TARANTULAS?

RANGE: all continents except Antarctica, but most are found in South America

HABITAT: rain forests, deserts, scrublands

HAIRY DEFENSE

The tarantula's legs (all eight of them) are covered with tiny hairs. Many tarantula species have special hairs on their abdomens and when frightened flick the hairs off with their legs.

Bird-eating Spider

SPINNING

Like other spiders, the tarantula makes a silken web, but not for catching dinner. Tarantulas make webs for their house, as a molting mat, or to help hold their food. For dinner, tarantulas ambush and run after their food.

Mexican Fireleg Tarantula

DIGESTING BEFORE EATING

After dark, the tarantula hunts a variety of insects, other spiders, and small lizards, snakes, and frogs. One bite releases venom that not only kills its dinner but begins to dissolve the victim's flesh.

A LOVE TO DIE FOR!

A male tarantula seeks a mate by following the scent of a female. The pair will perform a courtship dance and then, maybe, mate. Or, if the female is hungry, she might just eat the male instead.

So They Say!
A tarantula would rather hide from you than bite you.

TARANTULA'S WORST NIGHTMARE

When a female tarantula hawk (a large wasp) stings a tarantula and drags it into her burrow, the wasp lays a single egg on the body of the living spider. When the larva hatches, it eats the tarantula.

CHANGING CLOTHES

All tarantulas have a hard exoskeleton that they must shed during each growth spurt. When the time comes, the tarantula spins a silken mat and flips over onto its back. The "old" exoskeleton opens on the back, and the tarantula must push it off by expanding and contracting its body. When the process is complete, the spider lets the new exoskeleton harden, then turns right side up.

Chinese Newt

Amphibians

WHAT IN THE WORLD ARE AMPHIBIANS?

- live part of their lives in water and part on land
- cannot regulate temperature (are ectotherms)
- vertebrates (have a backbone)
- lay eggs, except fire salamander
- young do not look like parents
- go through metamorphosis

AMPHIBIAN STUFF

LARGEST: Japanese giant salamander, 6 feet

SMALLEST: Izecksohn's toad (also called gold frog), 0.39 inches

HEAVIEST: Japanese giant salamander, 140 pounds

LIGHTEST: Izecksohn's toad (also called gold frog), few grams

LONGEST LIFE SPAN: salamander, to 55 years

NUMBER OF SPECIES: 5,500 known

THREE GROUPS OF AMPHIBIANS

Caecilians. No arms or legs; look like large worms.

Salamanders, newts, and mud puppies. Small eyes, narrow heads, and have tails.

Frogs and toads. Young hatch as tadpoles with gills and tails.

Axolotl

Waxy Tree Frog

Green (Sonoran) Toad

Frog & Toad

Bornean Tree Frog

WHAT'S THE DIFFERENCE?

Frogs have long legs that are good for hopping, skin that is smooth and moist, and special pads on their toes that help them climb. Toads have shorter legs and drier skin, often with warty-looking bumps. Frogs are more likely to live in or near water.

Woodhouse's or Rocky Mountain Toad

WHERE IN THE WORLD ARE FROGS & TOADS?

RANGE: everywhere except Antarctica, the Arctic, and Greenland

HABITAT: every kind except polar regions and very dry deserts

Solomon Island Horned Frog

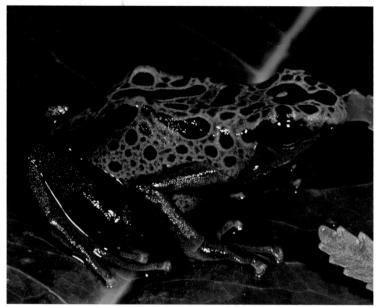
Blue Poison Arrow Frog

WHAT COLOR ARE YOU WEARING?
Brightly colored frogs (like poison dart frogs) are easy to see and warn potential predators that the frog is toxic. Frogs and toads who are green or brown are camouflaged so predators have a hard time spotting them.

Warning: Poison
Some poison dart frogs are so toxic that one drop of their skin secretion can kill an adult human.

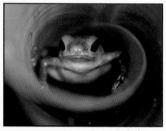
Blue-legged Poison Dart Frog

DON'T MESS WITH A TOAD
If a toad sees a predator, the toad puffs itself up so it looks too big to swallow. Most toads also secrete a burning milky toxin from a gland behind their eyes.

Cameroon Toad

NO-NECK
Most frog and toad species have large, protruding eyes to see in most directions. They also hop around to look in another direction. They cannot turn their heads since they don't have a neck.

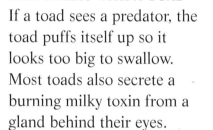
Red-eyed Tree Frog

WHAT'S FOR DINNER?

Most frogs and toads eat insects, spiders, worms, and slugs. They keep a large part of the world's insect population under control.

Bell's Horned Frog

Blomberg's Toad

WHERE'S THE HORNY TOAD?

Horny toads (horned toads) are not really toads, they're lizards. So you won't be learning about them here!

Warts
Can you get warts from holding a toad? No!

Smooth-sided Toad

Green (Sonoran) Toad

Green and Black Poison Arrow Frog

DAD TAKES THE LEAD

In many species of toads and frogs the dad cares for the eggs. He may take them to a safe, wet place by putting the eggs on his back, in his mouth, or in a pouch on his belly. Or he might wait until the eggs hatch into tadpoles before he moves them from a wet place on land to the water.

Argentine Horned Frog or Pacman Frog

EATING THE BABIES

The highly endangered Australian gastric-brooding frog has one of the weirdest ways to care for eggs. The female eats as many as 20 eggs and stops eating regular food because the eggs are developing in her stomach. When the eggs turn into tadpoles, she vomits them and starts eating again.

TADPOLES, POLYWOGS, AND FROGLETS

The mother frog or toad lays her eggs in water, or at least in a moist place. The eggs hatch into tadpoles that look like big-headed fish. Tadpoles grow legs, absorb their tails, lose their gills, and turn into frogs or toads that breathe air and hop.

Bornean Eared Frog

Waxy Tree Frog

Growing Legs
The hind legs of frogs and toads grow faster than their front legs.

WEATHER FORECASTERS

Before a rainstorm, spadefoot toads come out by the hundreds to croak something that sounds like, "Rain-today, rain-today."

Salamander & Newt

SALAMANDER & NEWT STUFF

LONGEST: Japanese giant salamander, 6 feet
SHORTEST: *Thorius arboreus*, 0.6 inches
HEAVIEST: giant salamander, 140 pounds
LIFE SPAN: to 55 years
NUMBER OF EGGS: 1 to 450
CONSERVATION STATUS: Lake Lerma salamander and Sardinian brook salamander at critical risk; many others endangered

Female Mandarin Newt

Female Mandarin Newt

WHAT'S THE DIFFERENCE?

Newts have smooth, slick skin and salamanders have dry, warty skin. But there are exceptions. A fire salamander's skin is smooth and damp, while crested newts shed their dry, warty skin when they return to the water to breed. But all salamanders and newts must keep their skin moist. If they get hot and dry, they die.

ALL LEGS

Salamanders' front legs grow faster than the back legs. But all four legs on a salamander (except for sirens) are so short that its belly drags on the ground.

FAT TOES, SHORT TOES

Some salamanders with four legs have fat toes. Other salamanders have webbed feet with very short toes to help them climb on slippery surfaces.

IS A NEWT A SALAMANDER?

A newt is a salamander but a salamander is not always a newt. Salamander is the name for an entire group, or scientific order, of amphibians that have tails as adults. This includes animals commonly known as newts and sirens.

WHERE IN THE WORLD ARE SALAMANDERS & NEWTS?

RANGE: North, Central, and South America; Europe, Africa, and Asia

HABITAT: ponds, swamps, streams, lakes, rivers, wet mountain forests, and grasslands

Axolotl

A SALAMANDER BY ANY OTHER NAME

Newts are salamanders that spend most of the year living on land. Sirens are salamanders that have lungs as well as gills and never develop beyond the larval stage. Other names given to salamanders include olm, axolotl, spring lizard, water dog, mud puppy, triton, and Congo eel.

WHERE ARE YOUR EARS?

Salamanders can't hear sounds, so they don't make any either. Some species hug the ground to pick up sound vibrations with their bodies.

LIZARD-FROG

Most salamanders look like a cross between a lizard and a frog. They have moist, smooth skin like frogs and long tails like lizards.

SMALL CLAWS

Only two salamander species have small, pointed claws on their toes: the long-tailed clawed salamander and the Japanese clawed salamander.

Chinese Giant Salamander

Oops, There Goes the Tail
Some salamanders shed their tails during an attack. But they will grow another one.

WHAT'S ON THE MENU?

All salamanders eat meat. Because they move slowly, salamanders eat slow-moving, soft-bodied creatures such as earthworms, slugs, and snails. Larger species of salamanders eat fish, crayfish, and small mammals such as mice and shrews. Salamanders sometimes hide and wait for a tasty meal to come close. Then the salamander snatches it. Some salamanders just flick out their tongues to catch dinner as it passes.

Chinese Newt

Female Mandarin Newt

LAND OR WATER OR BOTH?

Since salamanders need to stay cool and moist to survive, those that live on land are found in shady forested areas. They spend most of their time staying out of the sun under rocks and logs, up in trees, or in burrows they've dug in the damp earth. Some will seek out a pool of water where they can breed and lay their eggs before returning to the land. Others, like sirens and olms, spend their entire lives in the water.

Baby Blankets
Some mother newts keep their eggs safe by wrapping leaves around each one as they are laid—up to 400 eggs!

Fire Salamanders

Piercing Needles
The ribbed newt has needlelike ribs. When it squeezes its muscles, the ribs come through the newt's skin and sticks its enemy. Ouch!

BRINGING UP BABY

Most salamander species hatch from eggs. Female salamanders that live entirely in the water lay more eggs—up to 450—than those that spend some time on land.

MAMA NEEDED

The fire salamander is the only amphibian that does not hatch from an egg. Instead, the babies develop inside the mother's body.

YUCK!

Most salamanders, such as the red-spotted newt, have brightly colored but poisonous skin. That bright color tells other animals that the newt is not safe to eat. Many salamanders have glands on the back of the neck or on the tail that secrete a poisonous or bad-tasting liquid.

Tiger Salamander

CAVE-DWELLER
The only cave-dwelling amphibian is a salamander called an olm. Olms have very pale skin and have adapted to living in complete darkness in underground pools of water.

Bye-Bye
The California salamander stands up on its legs and waves its tail to scare away danger.

WHAT IS A SALAMANDER?
Most salamanders are small, most less than six inches long. Their heads are narrow and they have small eyes.

Axolotl

TAKE A DEEP BREATH
Sirens keep their gills all their lives and can breathe underwater. Others, such as the tiger salamander, develop lungs to breathe air. But most salamanders never develop lungs or gills. Lungless salamanders breathe through their skin and the thin membranes in the mouth and throat.

TWO-LEGGED SALAMANDER
One salamander, the siren, has no back legs but they have strong tails to make up for the lack of legs. When they swim, their long, flat tails flap from side to side like fish.

Pacific Giant Salamander

Komodo Dragon

Reptiles

WHAT IN THE WORLD ARE REPTILES?

- cannot regulate temperature (are ectotherms)
- some hibernate or enter a state of torpor in winter
- vertebrates (have a backbone)
- have scales on their bodies
- most lay eggs
- hatchlings look like small adults

REPTILE STUFF

LONGEST: reticulated python, 33 feet
HEAVIEST: saltwater crocodiles, 2,000 pounds (1.1 tons)
SHORTEST: dwarf gecko, 0.75 inch
LIGHTEST: dwarf gecko, 0.185 grains (120 milligrams)
FASTEST: six-lined racerunner, 18 miles per hour
LONGEST LIFE SPAN: tortoises, over 150 years
NUMBER OF SPECIES: more than 6,500

Anegada Ground Iguana

Baby Red Mountain Racer Snake with Eggs

Spider Tortoise

FOUR GROUPS OF REPTILES

Turtles and tortoises. Have a hard protective shell. Spend time in both water and on land, depending upon the species.

Lizards and snakes. Small head, short neck and long body, small or no legs.

Crocodiles and alligators. Spend most of their time in water, are carnivorous, and take care of their young.

Tuatara. A species left from an ancient group of reptiles that goes back to the dinosaurs.

Alligator & Crocodile

Slender-snouted Crocodile

American Alligator

African Dwarf Crocodile

IS IT AN ALLIGATOR OR A CROCODILE?

Alligators have wide, U-shaped, rounded snouts. Crocodiles have longer, more pointed, V-shaped snouts. Crocodiles live in saltwater habitats. Alligators live in freshwater habitats. If the fourth tooth on the lower jaw sticks up over the upper lip, it's a crocodile. Don't get too close looking for that tooth!

Say Ahhhhh!
A croc's tongue can't move. It's attached to the bottom of its mouth.

African Slender-snouted Crocodile

American Alligator

Slender-snouted Crocodile

That's a Croc!
All the species of alligators, caimans, crocodiles, and gharial together
are known as crocodilians or crocs.

African Slender-snouted Crocodile

WHAT'S FOR DINNER?
Crocs are carnivores and eat whatever they can catch in the
water or along the banks. They eat fish, turtles, frogs, birds, pigs,
deer, buffalo, and monkeys, depending on the size of the croc.

COME ON IN,
THE WATER'S FINE!
Crocs are most at home
in or near the water.
They look like logs
floating in a swamp or
washed up on shore.
Crocs can hold their
breath underwater for
more than an hour.

African Slender-snouted Crocodile

WHERE IN THE WORLD
?
ARE CROCS?

ALLIGATOR AND CAIMAN

RANGE: alligators, southern
United States and eastern
China; caimans, Central and
South America

HABITAT: grassy swamps and
slow-moving rivers

CROCODILE

RANGE: Mexico, Central and
South America, Africa,
Southeast Asia, and Australia

HABITAT: grassy swamps and
slow-moving rivers

Three-month-old Baby Alligator

WHAT'S THEIR STATUS?

Of the 23 crocodilian species, 12 are in need of conservation help. Many croc species were hunted for their skins to make shoes and luggage, and some have suffered from a loss of habitat. The American alligator was once considered endangered; but it has made a remarkable comeback.

MOTHER LOVE—CROC STYLE

Crocs take care of their babies for the first year of their life. Some species make a mound nest out of soil and plants; others dig a hole in the sandy beach. Then Mama croc lays her eggs and settles in to guard them from predators. When the babies start to hatch, they make grunting or barking noises from *inside the egg.* They use a tooth on the end of their snouts called an egg tooth to break out of the leathery eggshell. Some croc moms help by gently biting the egg to open it. After the young have hatched, Mom carries them to the water in her mouth. Sometimes the hatchlings ride on her back. In some croc species, Mama calls to the hatchlings to swim into her mouth for protection.

Juvenile American Alligator

American Alligator

I HAVEN'T EATEN IN YEARS!

All crocs store fat in their tails. Some big adults can go without eating for as long as two years!

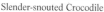

Slender-snouted Crocodile

Can You Outrun a Croc?

Crocs can swim up to 20 miles per hour. Those short legs can carry them up to 11 miles per hour for short distances.

Slender-snouted Crocodile

CROCODILE TEARS

Crocs do cry, but the only purpose of the tears is to get rid of excess salt in the croc's body.

How Did You Get So Big?

Crocodilians never stop growing!

Slender-snouted Crocodile Eye

CHEW EVERY BITE

Crocs don't chew their food. They tear off large chunks and swallow it or they swallow the prey whole. The croc juggles the food around until it's in the right position, then tosses its head back so the food falls down its throat.

COMING TO THEIR SENSES

Crocs hear through slits in their heads. When they dive into the water, the slits close to keep water out. Crocs have eyes on top of their heads so they can see as they cruise the water looking for food. They have good night vision because their vertical pupils open wider than round ones and let in more light. Crocs have taste buds to taste their food, and special organs in their snouts give them a great sense of smell.

Reptiles 45

...bian sand boa and elegant sand boa, both to 16 inches
HEAVIEST: anaconda, to 280 pounds
LIFE SPAN: to 35 years
NUMBER OF YOUNG AT BIRTH: 4 to 40
CONSERVATION STATUS: Round Island keel-scaled boa, Madagascar ground boa, and Madagascar tree boa endangered; many others vulnerable

Annulated Boa

PUTTING THE SQUEEZE ON DINNER

Boas are constrictors. They grab their prey with their teeth, coil their bodies around the prey, and squeeze and squeeze. They squeeze so tightly that the prey animal cannot breathe and it suffocates. The snake then unhinges its jaw and swallows the prey whole, usually headfirst.

It's the Truth!
Female anacondas grow much larger than the males.

JUST HANGIN' AROUND

Boas that live in a dry environment usually hang out in rock crevices or in underground burrows made by other animals. The ones that live in forests blend into the leaves on the ground to stay hidden. All in all, a boa would rather avoid people than go looking for trouble.

Green Anaconda

"WALK" A STRAIGHT LINE

Boas move by traveling forward in a straight line, which is known as rectilinear progression. They stiffen their ribs to provide support, then lift the scales on their belly, move the scales forward so the loose ends grip the surface and push the snake ahead. This type of movement works on the ground as well as in trees, and boas can even climb smooth surfaces. They are slow though, moving only about one mile per hour.

Emerald Tree Boa

Black-headed Python

Madagascar Ground Boa

LOOKING FOR A HOT MEAL

Boas eat rodents, birds, lizards, frogs, and small to medium-sized mammals like opossums, monkeys, pigs, or deer. Boas are ambush hunters. They hide, then they lie still until one of those tasty animals comes walking by. The boa quickly strikes to catch it. Yum, yum.

WHERE IN THE WORLD ARE BOAS?

RANGE: Western North America, Central and South America, Africa, Madagascar, western Asia, and Pacific Islands

HABITAT: rain forests, swamps, woodlands, grasslands, savannas, and semidesert scrublands

Solomon Island Boa

Madagascar Ground Boa

YOU'RE ON YOUR OWN, KIDS

Boas give birth to live young. When baby boas are born, they are surrounded by a protective membrane. Mom goes on her way while the babies break out of the membrane. This makes the babies so hungry that they then go look for something to eat.

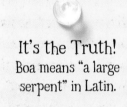

It's the Truth!
Boa means "a large serpent" in Latin.

BON APPÉTIT

Anacondas have been known to eat animals like caimans and young tapirs in the wild. Rhythmic muscular contractions pull the prey down the snake's throat and into its stomach. The snake has a special tube in the bottom of its mouth that remains open to one side to take in air so it can breathe while its mouth is full.

Babies of South American Boa Constrictor

Desert Rosy Boa

Pacific Rubber Boa

WHAT'S THAT SMELL?

Boas "smell" by flicking their tongues in and out. This way of smelling helps them find their dinner. Most boas also have special temperature-sensitive scales around their mouths that can sense the heat of a nearby animal.

A TASTY APPETIZER

Boa constrictors like to eat bats. They catch them by hanging from tree branches or the mouths of caves and knocking the bats out of the air as they fly by.

Boa Constrictor

Python

Carpet Python

WHERE IN THE WORLD ARE PYTHONS?

RANGE: Africa, Madagascar, Southeast Asia, and Australia

HABITAT: rain forests, grasslands, savannas, woodlands, and swamps

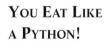
Timor Python

YOU EAT LIKE A PYTHON!
The rock python needs only enough food each year equal to its own weight. It eats this much in one meal!

Angolan Python

Burmese Python

WHAT'S IN THAT TREE?
Pythons do not jump out of trees onto animals below. Diving out of a tree can hurt a snake, especially a big one. Most big pythons stay on the ground.

Green Tree Python Hatching

Ball Python Brooding Eggs

Green Tree Python Hatchling

WATCHFUL MOMS

Pythons lay eggs. Some lay them in a shallow nest; others cover them with leaves and soil. Most python mothers coil around their eggs to protect them while they develop, which is called brooding. If the temperature drops, the mothers of larger species shiver to warm their eggs. But after the eggs hatch, it's "bye-bye, Mom." The babies are on their own.

NOT THE TOP OF THE FOOD CHAIN

Small, young pythons may be attacked and eaten by a variety of birds, mammals, frogs, insects, spiders, and even other snakes. Adult pythons are at risk from birds of prey, like eagles, and even lions and leopards.

My, What Big Teeth You Have!
Pythons have four rows of teeth in their upper jaw. They have fangs but do not produce venom.

COME ON IN, THE WATER'S FINE

Pythons spend a lot of time in the water. Often they lie beneath the surface of a stream or slow-moving river with only their heads above water. When a bird or small mammal comes to the water's edge, the python is ready to pounce.

Woma (Python)

Rattlesnake

Eastern Diamond Rattlesnake

Neotropical Rattlesnake

WHY ARE THEY CALLED *RATTLE*SNAKES?

Rattlesnakes have either a rattle or a partial rattle made of interlocking rings of keratin, the same material our fingernails are made of, at the end of their body. When vibrated, the rattles create a sound that warns off predators.

A FRIGHTENED SNAKE IS DANGEROUS
Snakes bite to defend themselves. If they are frightened, they try to escape or hide. Some keep still, depending on their camouflage, while others silently glide away. If they can't escape, they will hiss, rattle their tail, and puff up their body.

Aruba Island Rattlesnake

Neotropical Rattlesnake

WHERE IN THE WORLD ARE RATTLESNAKES?

RANGE: North and South America, mainly southwestern United States

HABITAT: mainly grasslands, scrublands, rocky hills, deserts, swamplands, and meadows

Just How Big Are They?
Most rattlesnake species are
two to four feet long.

Twin-spotted Rattlesnake

THEY KEEP COMING BACK HOME

Young rattlers leave their mothers when just a few weeks old. When it's time to hibernate in the winter, these youngsters follow their mother's scent and curl up in her den. Some dens have been used for over *100 years*!

I FEEL A DINNER COMING ON

Rattlesnakes are also called pit vipers because the heat-sensitive organ on each side of the head is known as a pit. A rattlesnake can detect prey that is as little as one-tenth of a degree warmer than their background.

Red Diamond Rattlesnake

NEVER FIGHT WITH A RATTLESNAKE!

Move away quickly if you see a rattlesnake. Never try to kill a snake. If you are bitten by a venomous snake, go to a hospital immediately!

BEWARE BABY RATTLESNAKES!

Rattlesnakes do not lay eggs. They give birth to live babies. Young rattlers are independent minutes after they are born. In some species their venom is more toxic than the adults' venom. At one to two weeks, they shed their skin. Each time they shed their skin, another segment of rattle is created.

Aruba Island Rattlesnake

THE RATTLESNAKE DIET

Rattlesnakes eat only when they are hungry. On average, an adult rattler eats only about once every two weeks. Younger rattlesnakes eat about once a week.

Living with Rattlers
Rattlesnakes are important to the environment because they control rodent populations. But watch where you step when out hiking!

DOING THE FREESTYLE

Who would guess that rattlesnakes are good swimmers? They have been found several miles out at sea!

Huamantlan Rattlesnake

Tortoise & Turtle

Leopard Tortoise

ALL FOR ONE, ONE FOR ALL

All turtles, tortoises, and terrapins are reptiles. They all have scales, lay eggs, and are ectothermic (cold blooded).

Stripe-necked Turtle

WHERE IN THE WORLD ARE TORTOISES & TURTLES?

RANGE: tortoises and turtles, temperate and tropical regions

HABITAT: aquatic species, oceans, swamps, freshwater lakes, ponds, and streams; terrestrial species, deserts, forests, and grasslands

Painted Terrapin

AT THE DAY SPA

Some turtles groom each other. One turtle uses its jaws to pull algae and loose pieces of shell off the other. Then they switch places and the other grooms the first.

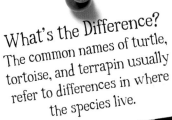
Roti Island Snake-naked Turtle

TURTLES

Turtles spend most of their lives in the water and most have webbed feet for swimming. Sea turtles are especially adapted for water, with flippers and a streamlined body shape. They rarely leave the ocean, except when females come ashore to lay their eggs. Other turtles live in freshwater, like ponds and lakes. They swim, but they also climb out onto banks, logs, or rocks to bask in the sun. In cold weather, they may burrow into the mud until spring brings warm weather.

TERRAPIN

Terrapins can live on land, but always beside rivers, ponds, and lakes. Terrapins are often found in swampy areas. The word terrapin comes from a Native-American word meaning "little turtle."

What's the Difference?
The common names of turtle, tortoise, and terrapin usually refer to differences in where the species live.

Painted Terrapin

TORTOISES

Tortoises live on land and eat low-growing shrubs, grasses, and even cactus. Their feet are round and stumpy. Tortoises that live in hot, dry habitats use their strong legs to dig burrows. When it's too hot in the sun, they go into the cooler underground.

Galápagos Tortoise

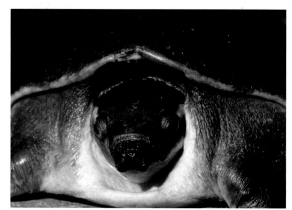

Indochinese Box Turtle

HOUSE ON LEGS
A turtle's shell is part of its skeleton. The turtle cannot crawl out of it, because the shell is permanently attached to the spine and the rib cage.

Ouch, That Hurt!
Turtles can feel pressure and pain through their shells, just as you can feel pressure through your fingernails.

WHAT ABOUT THAT SHELL?
Turtles and tortoises have hard, protective shells that are made up of 59 to 61 bones covered by plates called scutes. The shell's top is called the carapace, and the bottom is the plastron.

Asian Leaf Turtle

Fly River Turtle

A PLACE TO HIDE
Some turtles can pull their heads, legs, and feet inside their shells. Other turtles cannot pull their legs or heads into their shells.

Red-bellied Short-necked Turtle

MIGRATING TURTLES

Some sea turtles migrate thousands of miles through the sea on regular routes and return every two or three years to the same beaches to lay their eggs. No one knows how sea turtles find their way over that great distance, year after year, to the same beaches.

African Pancake Tortoise

WHAT'S FOR DINNER?

Most turtles and tortoises eat plants, fish, snails, worms, or insects. Others eat only grasses, leafy plants, flowers, fruits, and even cactus. Some are specialists: the leatherback sea turtle and the hawksbill turtle dine on jellyfish, even poisonous ones. Other turtles have broad, expanded jaws for crushing the shells of mollusks.

Galápagos Tortoise

African Spurred Tortoise

Leopard Tortoise Hatchling

BUILDING A NEST
All turtles and tortoises lay eggs, which they bury in soil, sand, or vegetation. Some species lay only a few oblong-shaped eggs; others lay 100 or more round eggs. Once the eggs are laid, the mother leaves.

Chinese Stripe-necked Turtle Hatchling

LEMME OUT OF HERE!
Hatchlings use an egg tooth to break out of the shell. After that, they have to find their own food. For many species, the temperature in the nest determines the sex of the hatchlings: warmer areas result in females, cooler areas result in males.

DIVING SUIT
The leatherback turtle's back is covered with leathery skin supported by tiny bones. This adaptation allows the turtle to dive up to 3,000 feet below the ocean surface. At this depth, the water pressure would crush a heavy shell and less flexible body.

Madagascar Flat-tailed Tortoise Baby

Desert Tortoise

Three-keeled Chinese Box Turtle

TURTLE SENSE

Turtles and tortoises do not have ears, but they can feel vibrations and changes in water pressure. They also have a good sense of smell. The skin of a turtle or tortoise, especially the land tortoises, looks leathery and tough but is actually very sensitive to touch.

Malaysian Giant Turtle

GONE FISHIN'

Many aquatic turtles use the "gape and suck" method to eat. They lie in wait for a fish to come by, open their mouths and throats wide, and suck in the fish.

Galápagos Tortoise

GALÁPAGOS TORTOISE STUFF

LENGTH: to 6 feet

WEIGHT: males, to 573 pounds; females, to 300 pounds

LIFE SPAN: more than 150 years

WEIGHT AT HATCHING: 3 ounces

CONSERVATION STATUS: endangered

WHEN IS A SHELL A SHELL?

The shell of the Galápagos tortoise is made of a honeycomb material that encloses small air chambers. If it were solid shell, it would be too heavy to carry.

WHERE IN THE WORLD ARE GALÁPAGOS TORTOISES?

RANGE: the Galápagos Islands, 600 miles west of Ecuador

HABITAT: open grassy areas

GUM YOUR FOOD WELL

Turtles and tortoises don't have teeth. They have a hard, sharpened edge in their mouth that they use to bite with, like a bird's beak. Some species also have a hard shelf, or secondary palate, in the upper jaw that helps them crush food.

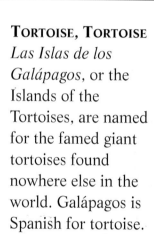

TORTOISE, TORTOISE

Las Islas de los Galápagos, or the Islands of the Tortoises, are named for the famed giant tortoises found nowhere else in the world. Galápagos is Spanish for tortoise.

DON'T TIP OVER!

The shell is attached to the tortoise's ribs. The tortoise's lungs are located on the top of its body, under the top dome of the shell. If the tortoise is flipped over, the weight of its body can crush its lungs.

So Long, Baby

Females travel several miles to reach their nesting area of dry, sandy ground. The female digs a hole about 12 inches deep and lays hard-shelled eggs the size of tennis balls. She covers them with sand, and then she leaves. When the young tortoises hatch, they must dig their way to the surface. This might take a whole month! Then they're on their own.

Galápagos Adult and Hatchling

Galápagos Hatchling

What's for Dinner?

Tortoises eat prickly pear cactus and fruits, as well as flowers, water ferns, leaves, and grasses. Galápagos tortoises store food and water in their body and can go without eating or drinking for up to a year!

Can't You Walk a Little Faster?

Galápagos tortoises amble along at 0.16 miles per hour. Humans walk at an average speed of 2.8 miles per hour.

STRETCH THAT NECK!

When male tortoises fight, they face each other, open their mouths, and stretch their heads as high as they can. Whoever stretches highest wins.

WHAT A LIFE!

Giant tortoises spend all day grazing, lying in the sun, or wallowing in puddles. Because they are cold-blooded, they warm up in the sun. On cool nights, they partially submerge themselves in mud, water, or brush to keep warm.

Lizards

Green Crested Basilisk

IT'S ON THE TIP OF MY TONGUE!
The Madagascan chameleon has a sticky-tipped tongue which it can shoot out farther than the length of its body!

LIZARD ON YOUR FINGER
The smallest reptile in the world—dwarf gecko—can fit on the tip of your finger!

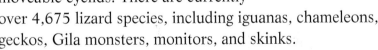

Madagascar Giant Day Gecko

WHAT IS A LIZARD?
In general, lizards have a small head, short neck, and long body and tail. And unlike snakes, most lizards have moveable eyelids. There are currently over 4,675 lizard species, including iguanas, chameleons, geckos, Gila monsters, monitors, and skinks.

Do You Hear a Cricket?
Geckos make chirping and clicking noises to defend their territory or attract a mate.

New Caledonian Rough-nosed Gecko

Sungazer

SLEEP ALL DAY, PLAY ALL NIGHT

Desert-dwelling lizards, like the ground gecko, usually sleep during the day under the warm sand, then come out when the sun has gone down.

OUCH, OUCH, OUCH!

To protect its feet from the hot sand, the sand lizard "dances" by lifting its legs up quickly, one at a time, or by resting its belly on the sand and lifting up all four legs at once!

San Diego Horned Lizard

Panther Chameleon

Spring Break

Marine iguanas spend much of their lives underwater. They sometimes come out of the water, however, to rest on a sandy beach.

DADDY NO-LEGS

Lizards that live in burrows have smaller legs than other lizards, or none at all. They can slither underground more easily than if they had long legs.

LIZARD HOMES

Some lizards live in trees. Tree dwellers have special toes and often a prehensile tail for grasping thin branches.

WHERE IN THE WORLD ARE LIZARDS?

RANGE: southern Canada to the tip of South America, most of Europe and Asia, and all of Africa and Australia

HABITAT: all habitats except extreme cold and deep oceans

That's Fast!

The six-lined racerunner holds the record for the fastest speed reached by any reptile on land: 18 miles per hour.

Parson's Chameleon Grabbing Worm

LOOKING FOR LUNCH

Most lizards eat insects, grabbing crickets, flies, grasshoppers, and more with long, sticky tongues or quick bites.

YUM, SMELL THAT TASTE

Lizards smell with their tongues. Like snakes, a lizard sticks out its tongue to catch scent particles in the air, then pulls back its tongue and places those particles on the roof of its mouth where there are special sensory cells.

Caiman Lizard

Jamaican Iguana

EH, WHAT DID YOU SAY?

Lizards don't have ear flaps like mammals do. Their ear openings catch sound, and lizard eardrums are just below the surface of their skin. But lizards cannot hear as well as humans.

Bamboo Leaf-tailed Gecko

DIG THAT COLOR!

Many lizards, such as iguanas, can see in color. Their colorful bodies allow them to communicate with each other, and help them tell who's male and who's female.

SOMETHING IN YOUR EYE?

Most lizards have eyelids that clean and protect their eyes when they blink. But some lizards, like geckos, can't blink. They have a clear membrane that shields their eyes from dirt or bright sun.

Fiji Island Banded Iguana

Fijian Iguanas

OFF WITH THE OLD!

Lizards have dry, scaly skin that does not grow with their bodies. Lizards shed, or molt, their old skin in large flakes to make way for the new skin growth underneath.

Madagascan Giant Day Gecko

THE GREAT ESCAPE

Several types of lizards are able to escape from an enemy by breaking off part of their tails. The tail will grow back over time, but it won't look the same.

Fernand's Skink

SCALES OF ALL KIND

Lizards' scales vary, depending on their habitat. Skinks have smooth scales so mud won't cling to them; others have bony plates under their scales for added protection from rough terrain.

Stay Away!

Horned lizards squirt blood from tiny blood vessels in their eyes to scare away enemies.

YOU LOOK SO FRILLY

The Australian frilled lizard has a ruffle of loose skin around its neck that sticks out when the lizard is frightened and makes the lizard look much bigger than it is.

Frilled Lizard

Iguana

Anegada Ground Iguana

Anegada Ground Iguana

Fijian Iguana Baby

WHERE IN THE WORLD ARE IGUANAS?

RANGE: from southeastern Canada to Central and South America, the Galápagos Islands, some Caribbean islands (such as Cuba, Jamaica, and the Anegadas), Fiji, and Madagascar

HABITAT: tropical and subtropical forests, deserts, and seashores

Green Iguana

Anegada Iguana Hatchling

BYE-BYE, BABIES

The females of most iguanas dig a burrow in a sunny area, lay 20 to 40 eggs, cover them up, then Mom heads for home. When the eggs hatch, the young dig out of the burrow.

Tastes Like Chicken

People of Central and South America eat the native green iguanas. They are called GALLINA DE PALO, or "chicken of the tree."

WHAT'S FOR DINNER?

Most iguanas eat fruits, flower buds, and young leaves. Some species also eat the occasional juicy mealworm or wax worm.

Cuban Rock Iguana

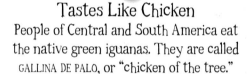
Jamaican Iguana

Komodo Dragon

KOMODO DRAGON STUFF

LENGTH: males, to 10 feet; females, to 8 feet
WEIGHT: to 176 pounds
LIFE SPAN: over 50 years
NUMBER OF EGGS: 15 to 30
SIZE AT HATCHING: 12 inches
CONSERVATION STATUS: endangered

GOOD LUCK, KIDS— YOU'RE ON YOUR OWN!

Mama dragon digs a nest, lays between 15 and 30 eggs, then scrambles away. After eight or nine months, the babies hatch. They immediately scramble up the nearest tree so they won't be eaten by the adult dragons. Fortunately, the adults are too heavy to climb trees. Youngsters live in the trees eating eggs, grasshoppers, beetles, and geckos until they are about four years old and four feet long. Then these teenagers are ready to try life on the ground.

WHAT IN THE WORLD IS A KOMODO DRAGON?

The Komodo dragon is an ancient species of reptile with ancestors that date back more than 100 million years. These large lizards have stubby, bowed legs, clay-colored, scaly skin, and a huge, muscular tail. The Komodo's long, forked tongue is yellow.

WHERE IN THE WORLD ARE KOMODO DRAGONS?

RANGE: Indonesia

HABITAT: hot grasslands and tropical forests

I Can't Believe I Ate the Whole Thing!

The Komodo dragon can consume up to 80 percent of its body weight during *one meal*.

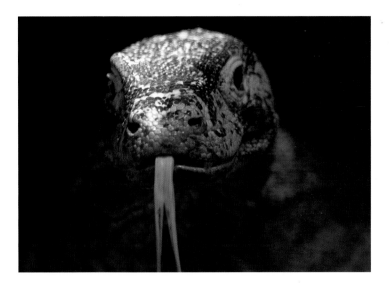

Dentists Needed

Dragons have 60 short, sharp teeth to cut and tear flesh. A dragon will go through four or five *sets* of teeth in a lifetime.

Looking for a Warm Meal—or Cold Leftovers

Komodo dragons can smell dinner a mile away through their long tongues. They eat wild pigs, deer, wild buffalo, snakes, and fish that wash up on the shore. A dragon hides and waits for dinner to walk by. The dragon attacks, scratching and biting. Its bite contains deadly bacteria that will eventually kill its meal. So if dinner gets away, the dragon follows it until it drops. Then other dragons smell dinner and come running, sort of. Naturally, they all scratch and bite each other fighting for dinner.

A Life of Leisure

Each morning, the Komodo dragon climbs out of its burrow in the ground and looks for a sunny spot to warm up. Once warm, it's off to find breakfast, followed by a nice long nap in the shade during the hottest part of the day. Late in the afternoon, the dragon looks for dinner. After eating, it's bedtime and into the burrow until morning. Komodo dragons live and hunt alone.

Heavyweight Champion of the World!

The Komodo dragon is the biggest lizard in the world

Gang Gang Cockatoos

Birds

WHAT IN THE WORLD ARE BIRDS?

- regulate temperature (are endotherms)
- vertebrates (have a backbone)
- have feathers on their bodies
- lay hard-shell eggs
- have some hollow bones

BIRD STUFF

LARGEST: male ostrich, to 9 feet
SMALLEST: bee hummingbird, 2 inches
HEAVIEST: ostrich, 340 pounds
LIGHTEST: bee hummingbird, 0.05 ounces
FASTEST: white-throated spine-tail swift, 110 miles per hour
LONGEST LIFE SPAN: sulphur-crested cockatoo, 80 years
NUMBER OF SPECIES: more than 8,800 known

Greater Sulphur-Crested Cockatoo

TWO KINDS OF BIRDS

Precocial. The chicks of some bird species are covered with down when they hatch and can start finding their own food. Chickens are precocial.

Altricial. Other chicks hatch with no feathers, are helpless, and depend on their parents to feed them. Robins are altricial.

California Condor

Ostrich

California Condor

Condor with Puffed Out Throat

BALD IS BEAUTIFUL

Adult California condors have distinctive pink, bald heads that keep rotting food from sticking to them as they eat. The skin on the bare heads of adults turns a deep pink during courtship or when the birds are excited or alarmed. The adults also have a throat sack they puff out during courtship displays.

Did I Hear a Bird?
California condors do not have vocal chords, so they only make hissing and grunting noises.

NEAT FREAKS

After eating, the condor cleans its head and neck by rubbing against grass, rocks, or branches. Condors bathe frequently and spend hours smoothing and drying their feathers. They have a very hardy and effective immune system, so they don't get sick from any of the bacteria on the decaying animals they eat.

WHERE IN THE WORLD ARE CALIFORNIA CONDORS?

RANGE: currently only in isolated areas of reintroduction—California and Arizona in the United States, and Baja California, Mexico

HABITAT: wooded mountains and scrublands

THE ORIGINAL THUNDERBIRD

California condors are one of the largest flying birds. At one time there were thousands of them in the wild, ranging across the western United States and into Mexico. Native American tribes have great respect for the condor and see it as a symbol of power. They call it the thunderbird because they believe it brings thunder to the skies with the beating of its huge wings.

All Thumbs

Condors do not have talons like hawks or eagles. Their nails are more like blunt claws. They cannot grasp or carry prey with their feet.

BORN TO FLY

In flight, California condors are a wonder to behold. The triangular patch of white flashes under each huge wing. The condors ride the thermal air currents for hours, soaring through the skies as they scan the fields below. They reach speeds of up to 55 miles per hour and soar to altitudes of 15,000 feet.

California Condor Chick Hatching

NATURE'S CLEANUP CREW

California condors are vultures; and like all vultures, they feed on carrion (dead animals). Condors prefer large dead animals like deer, cattle, and sheep; but they also eat dead rodents, rabbits, and even fish. They don't have a good sense of smell like turkey vultures, so they find their food mostly by their keen eyesight. These large birds gorge themselves on two to three pounds of food at a time, and can then go without food for several days until they find another carcass.

A HOME IN THE CLIFFS

The adult female lays a single white or pale green-blue egg between January and March in a rock crevice or inside a cave in the rocky cliff. After incubating 54 to 68 days, the chick begins to hatch. It can take up to a week for a condor chick to break out of its egg. The chick has bare patches on its head, neck, belly, and underwing. At about eight weeks old, the chick will wander outside of its nest. By five or six months, the youngster is ready to practice flying.

Cockatoo

COCKATOO STUFF

TALLEST: red-tailed black cockatoo, 20 to 26 inches

SHORTEST: Solomon corella and Philippine cockatoo, 12 inches

HEAVIEST: palm cockatoo, 19.4 to 35.3 ounces

LIGHTEST: cockatiel, 2.8 to 3.5 ounces

LIFE SPAN: 40 to 60 years

CONSERVATION STATUS: Philippine cockatoo and lesser sulphur-crested cockatoo at critical risk

Salmon-crested Cockatoo

Cockatiel

Aru Great Black or Palm Cockatoo

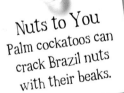

Nuts to You
Palm cockatoos can crack Brazil nuts with their beaks.

TOGETHER FOREVER

Cockatoos mate for life. Pairs work together to build their nests in tree hollows, filling them with leaves or wood chips. In many cases, both the male and the female incubate the eggs and care for the chicks. Cockatoos often stay with the flock in which they were raised.

WHERE IN THE WORLD ARE COCKATOOS?

RANGE: Australia, New Guinea, Indonesia, Solomon Islands, and Philippines

HABITAT: rain forests, scrublands, and savannas

Two-Stepping

Like all parrots, cockatoos can use their feet much like we use our hands. Cockatoos can easily climb through tree branches, where they find their primary diet of fruit and nuts. They are able to hold their food in one foot while balancing on the other.

Western Red-tailed Black Cockatoo

Love Those Beetles

Most cockatoos eat nuts, seeds, and fruit, but short-billed black-cockatoos and yellow-tailed black cockatoos feed on wood-boring beetle larvae.

Gang-gang Cockatoo

You're a Loudmouth!
Cockatoos are loud and noisy—probably the loudest of all the parrots. They scream to communicate with one another or just for the sheer joy of making noise.

On Guard

When feeding, cockatoos depend on fellow cockatoo guards that sit close to the feeding flock and keep an eye open for danger. Should a threat arise, the guard sends out a loud alarm and the entire flock takes flight, squawking and screaming.

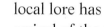

Red-tailed Black Cockatoo

The Rainmaker

In some areas of Australia, local lore has it that the arrival of the red-tailed black cockatoo means that rain is on the way; so the birds are a welcome sight.

Black (Yellow-tailed) Cockatoo

Harpy Eagle

HARPY EAGLE STUFF

LENGTH: 35 to 41 inches

WINGSPAN: to 7 feet

WEIGHT: male, 8.5 to 12 pounds;
female, 14 to 20 pounds

LIFE SPAN: 25 to 35 years

NUMBER OF EGGS: 1 to 2

CONSERVATION STATUS: lower risk

BOLD AND BEAUTIFUL

The harpy eagle has feathers on the top of its head that fan into a bold crest when the bird feels threatened. Some smaller feathers create a facial disk that may focus sound waves to improve the hearing.

Till Death Do You Part
Harpy eagles mate for life.

IT'S A MYTH

Early South American explorers named the harpy eagle after *Harpyja*, the predatory half-woman, half-bird monster of Greek mythology!

WHERE IN THE WORLD ARE HARPY EAGLES?

RANGE: southern Mexico to northern Argentina

HABITAT: rain forests

Harpy Hunting Grounds

Harpies are experts at saving energy. A harpy eagle never soars over the top of a rain forest. They hunt in and below the rain forest canopy. Harpies perch silently for hours—up to 23 hours!—in a tree, waiting to drop on unsuspecting prey.

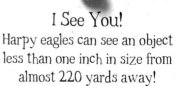

I See You!
Harpy eagles can see an object less than one inch in size from almost 220 yards away!

What's on the Menu?

The powerful harpy eagle flies low over the forest and uses its great talons to snatch up monkeys and sloths that can weigh up to 17 pounds! Harpies also feed on opossums, porcupines, young deer, snakes, and iguanas. Heavier prey is taken to a stump or low branch and partially eaten, since it is too heavy to be carried whole to the nest.

A World Turned Upside Down

The harpy eagle can turn its head *upside down* to get a better look at its potential meal.

Conservation

The massive harpy eagle looks invincible. But years of hunting, in addition to logging, destruction of nesting sites, and poaching have eliminated this bird species from much of its former range, especially the northern part, and it is now rare in many areas. Harpy parents raise, at most, a single eaglet every two years, so once the number of harpy eagles in a particular area has been reduced, it is hard for the population to recover.

Ten-week-old Harpy Eagle Chick

LIVING THE HIGH LIFE

Harpies build their nests 90 to 140 feet high in silk-cotton trees (kapok trees). They create a huge frame from large sticks, then line the nest with soft greens, seedpods, and animal fur to make it warm and comfortable. When finished, the nest will be about four feet thick and five feet across! A person could lie down in this nest! The eagle pair will use the nest for many years, sometimes even remodeling it.

THE STRONG, SILENT TYPE

Harpy eagles do not vocalize much; they wail (*wheeeeeee, wheeeeooooo*), croak, whistle, click, and mew.

Harpy Eagle on Nest

Harpy Eagle Pair at Nest with Eggs

IT'S SO HARD TO LEAVE HOME

The mother harpy eagle lays one or two eggs but when one chick hatches, the parents ignore the other egg and it dies. Both parents feed the eaglet for about 10 months. Harpy eagle chicks are ready to fledge at about six to seven months of age, but they hang around the nest for over a year, begging a meal from mother and father. As the parents provide less and less food, by returning to the nest only about every 10 days, Junior is forced to fend for himself. Harpy eaglets are so fond of their childhood homes that mature harpy eagles often return to build their own nest in their "home tree."

Phantom Bird
Few people have actually seen a harpy eagle in the wild.

RAIN FOREST TAKE-OUT

A harpy eagle finds most of its food in the rain forest canopy and understory instead of on the forest floor. When hunting, the eagle dives down onto its prey and snatches it with outstretched feet. Its short, broad wings help the harpy fly almost straight up, so it can attack prey from below as well as above. The larger females look for sloths and monkeys; the smaller, more agile, and faster males take smaller prey. This increases the pair's odds of eating on a regular basis.

You Can't Outrun a Harpy
Flying below the canopy, harpy eagles can fly up to 50 miles per hour.

SUCCESS AT THE ZOO

In 1994, the San Diego Zoo became the first facility in North America to hatch and successfully rear a harpy eagle. They currently have the only breeding pair of harpy eagles in North America.

SUPER EAGLE!

Harpies are not the largest bird of prey (that title belongs to the Andean condor), but they are definitely the heaviest and most powerful of birds of prey. Like most eagle species, the female harpy is almost twice as large as the male. The harpy eagle's legs can be as thick as a small child's wrist. Their curved talons are five inches long, longer than grizzly bear claws!

Crane

BALLET OF THE CRANES

All cranes, young and old alike, participate in elaborate, enthusiastic dancing, often just for the fun of it. In a flock of cranes, once a dance starts, it becomes contagious, with all the cranes joining in. Cranes will bow, leap, run, and have short flights during the dance. The cranes will pick up sticks, grass, feathers, or whatever small objects with their bills and toss them up into the air.

West African Crowned Crane

Crowned Crane

Make a Flying Leap

Not only is the sarus crane the tallest of the crane species, it is also the tallest flying bird!

ELEGANCE AND GRACE

Cranes are large birds with long necks and legs, streamlined bodies, and long, rounded wings. Cranes are some of the tallest birds in the world. In flight, their bodies form a straight line from their bills to their toes, presenting a beautiful, elegant image.

WATCH OUT FOR AIRPLANES

The Eurasian cranes fly over the Himalaya Mountains at 32,800 feet. That's cruising altitude for jets! The demoiselle cranes fly through the passes of the Himalaya mountains.

WHERE IN THE WORLD ARE CRANES?

RANGE: North America, Africa, Europe, Asia, and Australia

HABITAT: wetlands and grasslands

Sandhill Crane

THE FRENCH CONNECTION

Queen Marie Antoinette of France gave the dainty demoiselle crane its name. *Demoiselle* means maiden, or young lady, in French. The queen was enchanted by the crane's delicate and maidenly appearance.

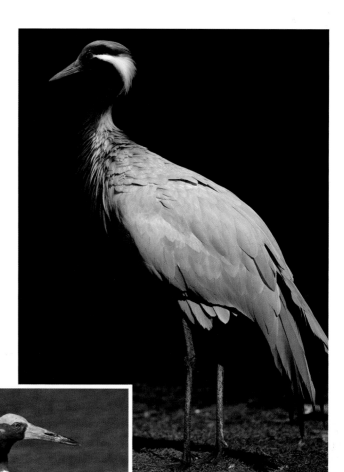

Demoiselle Crane

PACK YOUR BAGS

Siberian cranes, sandhill cranes, Eurasian cranes, whooping cranes, and demoiselle cranes migrate for the winter season. They fly at an altitude of 6,500 feet, form a V, and glide along. They call to each other constantly. Whooping cranes fly as far as 500 miles a day (186 miles is the average for all cranes). The lesser sandhill crane flies from eastern Siberia across the Bering Sea into North America and as far south as northern Mexico.

Indian Sarus Crane

BACK FROM THE BRINK

Whooping cranes are the tallest birds in North America and were once numerous in the prairie wetlands of the United States and Canada. Today, there are only 200 birds left in one wild flock and 85 left in a non-migratory flock.

NO PICKY EATERS

Cranes eat everything from snails to acorns to insects to snakes, and they change their eating habits depending on what is available. Shorter-billed cranes will eat insects as well as graze on grasses. Long-billed cranes will probe in shallow wetlands for crustaceans and other aquatic life. The bigger crane species have large, powerful bills and dig up roots and tubers out of the muddy wetlands.

Red-crowned Crane

Red-crowned Crane

A, B, C for Crane

Ancient Greeks believed the flight of cranes inspired the god Hermes to invent the Greek alphabet.

Ancient History

Fossils of crowned cranes show their existence 37 to 54 million years ago. Prehistoric cave paintings of cranes have been found in Europe, Africa, and Australia.

THEY GROW UP SO QUICKLY!

Sandhill crane chicks start swimming when they are only six hours old. Crane chicks also begin to learn crane language as soon as they hatch. After one year, the chick will know at least six calls and its voice will be deeper, louder, and stronger.

Crane Chick

WHERE'S MY DINNER?

Parents feed crane chicks almost immediately after they hatch. Sometimes, adults will feed chicks until they are several months old. The chicks grow very, very quickly and soon learn to follow their parents to food sources.

LEARN THE LANGUAGE

Cranes have a varied system of communication. Tone and volume changes with the species. Crowned cranes give soft honks; Siberian cranes sound like flutes. The call of a whooping crane can be heard a mile away.

White-naped Crane

West African Crowned Crane

Read My Body; Hear Me Roar
Cranes communicate with body language. Here's what a crane is "saying":

"I'M COMING AFTER YOU." The crane stands tall with body feathers smooth, head features expanded. It walks stiffly, flaps its wings, ruffles, bows, falsely preens, stomps, snorts, and growls.

"STAY AWAY!" The crane raises the feathers of its neck, wings, and back, partially opens and lowers its wings, ruffles them alternately, then lowers its bill in a preening movement, finishing with a low growl.

"KEEP AWAY FROM ME." The crane bends its legs, lowers to the ground, folds its wings loosely against its body and the ground, and places its head forward with the red patch prominent.

"OK, YOU'RE THE BOSS." The crane lowers its head and head feathers and walks in a loose and wary way.

Bald Eagle

Bald Eagle Stuff

Length: 29 to 42 inches

Wingspan: 5.5 to 8 feet

Weight: males, 6 to 9 pounds; females, 10 to 15 pounds

Life span: 25 to 40 years

Number of eggs: 1 to 3

Conservation status: threatened in southern Canada and most of the United States; abundant in its northern range, especially Alaska

Are Bald Eagles Really Bald?

Bald eagles' heads are covered with short white feathers. They are sometimes called American eagles, fishing eagles, Washington eagles, or white-headed eagles.

Our National Symbol

To symbolize the United States, the founders chose the bald eagle, a bird of prey found only in North America. Benjamin Franklin thought it was a poor choice because it sometimes steals food from other birds. He recommended the wild turkey.

Speed Freak

A bald eagle can reach a speed of up to 200 miles per hour when diving through the air to grab a meal.

EAGLE EYE

Bald eagles can see four to seven times better than humans. They are able to see things sharply from quite far away. This, of course, helps them spot their next meal from high in the sky, or from a lofty perch in a tree or on a cliff ledge. Unlike our eyes, an eagle's eyes cannot move from side to side. To look around, the eagle turns its whole head.

Balancing Act

When a bald eagle loses a feather on one wing, it will lose a matching one on the other. This way it stays balanced.

WHERE IN THE WORLD ARE BALD EAGLES?

RANGE: Canada, United States, and northwest Mexico

HABITAT: coastlines, lakes, rivers, swamps, and marshes

FALLING FOR EACH OTHER

It is believed that bald eagles choose a mate for life. To impress each other, a male and female perform a dance in the sky. They lock on to each other's talons and tumble and twist in the air. At the last second they let go, just before reaching the ground.

GONE FISHIN'

Bald eagles have spiny scales and sharp talons on their toes for gripping slippery fish and keen eyes to see one. A hungry eagle perches on a tree above the water until it spies a fish near the surface. Then it swoops down and plucks the fish out of the water. The eagle flies back to its nest and, with its powerful, hooked beak, rips into its food.

HOME, SWEET NEST

The bald eagle is a master nest builder. A pair of eagles build their large nest high in a sturdy tree or sometimes on the ground if no tree is around. Year after year, they return to the same nest and add twigs, grass, moss, feathers, and branches to the original nest until it becomes huge. Sometimes a nest gets so heavy that its supporting branches break, and the nest comes crashing down.

AND BABY MAKES THREE OR FOUR OR MORE!

After the nest is just right, the female will lay one to three eggs, each several days apart. Both parents will take turns keeping the eggs warm until they hatch. It takes both parents to care for the chicks. Mom eagle does most of the chick-sitting, but dad provides the food for his growing family.

IT'S TOUGH TO BE AN EAGLET

The first eaglet to hatch has several days to grow before its brothers and sisters hatch. This eaglet will get such a head start on its siblings that it will fight for the most food from the parents and may even kill its smaller, younger siblings. This ensures that at least one chick will survive to adulthood.

WHERE'S THE WHITE HEAD?

Upon hatching, baby eaglets are fluffy and light gray. Just prior to leaving the nest, at about 12 weeks old, the youngsters' feathers turn dark brown. The distinctive white head and neck feathers won't appear until maturity.

THE BALD EAGLE'S WORST ENEMY

Bald eagles are at the top of the food chain, so they have no natural enemies. When they become endangered, it's because of us humans. In the last century, pesticides used on farms contaminated the lakes from which the eagles got their food. Eagles became endangered. Now the pesticide use is regulated and bald eagles have made a dramatic comeback in some states.

Watch Your Plate!
When fish are scarce, bald eagles hunt rabbits, squirrels, other birds, and even young deer. They have also been known to steal food from other birds.

Flamingo

THE MORE THE MERRIER

Flamingos are social birds that live in groups of a few pairs to thousands or even tens of thousands. In East Africa, more than one million flamingos may gather together, forming the largest flocks of birds known.

THINK PINK AND ORANGE

The flamingos' pink or reddish color comes from the rich sources of carotenoid pigments (like the pigments in carrots) in the algae and small crustaceans that they eat. The Caribbean flamingos are the brightest, showing their true colors of red, pink, or orange on their legs, bills, and bodies.

UP, UP, AND AWAY

In order to fly, flamingos must run to gather speed, usually into the wind. In flight, flamingos stretch out their long necks and long legs. Their wings show black and red (or pink) coloration. When flying, flamingos flap their wings rapidly and almost continuously. They usually fly in large flocks and follow each other closely, taking advantage of the wind.

WHERE IN THE WORLD ARE FLAMINGOS?

RANGE: Africa, Asia, the Americas, and Europe

HABITAT: large, shallow lakes or lagoons

Adult Flamingo Sitting on Nest

HOME IS IN THE MUD

A flamingo nest is just a mound of mud, about 12 inches high. The nest needs to be high enough to protect the egg from flooding and from the occasional intense heat at ground level. Both the male and female build the nest by pulling mud toward them with their bills. Flamingos lay a single large egg, which is kept warm by both parents. At hatching, a flamingo chick has gray down. It also has a straight, pink bill and pink legs, both of which turn black within a week.

A Place of Their Own

When the young birds leave the nest, they herd together in large groups, called creches.

FOOD FOR THOUGHT

The flamingo's bill is held upside down in the water. The flamingo feeds by sucking water and mud in at the front of its bill and then pumping it out again at the sides, trapping shrimp and other small water creatures in the flamingo's mouth.

Rest Awhile

Standing on one leg is the flamingo's most comfortable resting position.

GOT MILK?

After hatching, the chick stays in the nest for five to 12 days. During this time, the chick is fed crop milk that comes from the parents' upper digestive tract. The mother, the father, and other flamingos feed the chick. The begging calls from the hungry chick stimulates the secretion of the milk.

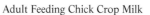
Adult Feeding Chick Crop Milk

Hummingbird

Anna's Hummingbird, Male

Costa's Hummingbird

SPLISH, SPLASH, I'M TAKING A BATH

Hummingbirds like to take baths several times a day. They bathe by splashing in shallow water or sitting near a waterfall or a sprinkler and letting the spray fall on them. A few even dive in and out of water and then shake their feathers and preen themselves with their bills and claws.

Giant Hummingbird

WHY WALK WHEN YOU CAN FLY?

The hummingbird is fearless, because it can outmaneuver everything, unless it is taken by surprise. Like a helicopter, a hummingbird can go up, down, sideways, backwards, even upside down. They can beat their wings up to 200 times per minute. Hummingbirds are such good fliers that most of them never walk more than two inches at a time.

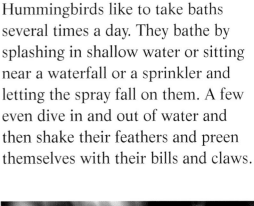

WHERE IN THE WORLD ARE HUMMINGBIRDS?

RANGE: North, Central, and South America

HABITAT: all, wherever suitable food plants occur

BOMBS AWAY!

If a hummingbird sees a hawk or other bird in its territory, it will give a high-pitched warning then start dive-bombing it. Other hummers and even birds of different species often join in to dive-bomb the hawk until they chase it away.

Anna's Hummingbird

AMAZING APPETITES

Hummingbirds are small in size, but they have large appetites. They need lots of calories because of their high heart rate and small body size. Thousands of plants rely on hummingbirds for pollination.

Speed Record
One of the fastest birds is the green violet-ear hummingbird. It can fly up to 93 miles per hour for short distances.

WHO'S HUMMING?

Hummingbirds include the smallest birds in the world, but they belong to one of the largest families of birds. Hummingbirds are found in deserts, on mountains, and on plains, but most are found in the tropical rain forests. Their name refers to the humming sound made by their tiny beating wings.

Oasis Hummingbird and Nest

NEED A STRAW

The hummingbird's long slender bill is adapted for collecting nectar from flowers. The bill protects the bird's long, split tongue and allows each kind of hummingbird to feed from specific types of flowers. Ninety percent of all hummingbirds' diet is nectar from flowers. They also snack on insects now and then, which they catch by diving to snap the insect out of the air.

Costa's Hummingbird

Costa's Hummingbird

OH BABY, BABY

Hummingbird babies are blind when they hatch; they have a little down on their bodies and bumps for bills. These tiny chicks are very vulnerable, and their predators include large insects. Fortunately, their mothers are very protective.

Macaw

Hyacinth Macaw

SCREECH, SQUEAL, AND SQUAWK

Screaming is a natural behavior for macaws. They do it to make contact with one another, to define territory, and sometimes just for fun. Loud screeching and squawking voices help make their presence known in dense rain forests. They can also imitate sounds and words that they hear, often practicing to themselves until they get it right.

Zooming Around

Macaws have a streamlined body and wings that don't flap deeply. The red-fronted macaw can fly at up to 40 miles per hour.

THE FAMILY THAT FLOCKS TOGETHER

Macaws live in pairs, family groups, or flocks of 10 to 30. Before dawn, the flock awakens, preens their feathers, and calls to one another. They fly to the day's feeding grounds—a grove of trees with ripe fruit. They feast until midday, when they settle down for a rest. In the afternoon they eat again until close to dusk.

MUSICAL CHAIRS

At dusk, flocks of macaws return to their roosting site, where they call to each other to figure out who sits where. The sitting arrangement can change from day to day. Sometimes squabbles break out, but macaws rarely injure each other. Once everyone is settled, they quiet down, fluff out their feathers, and prepare to snooze through the night.

Scarlet Macaw

A SPLASH OF COLOR

The macaws' brightly colored feathers blend in with the green leaves, red and yellow fruits, and bluish shadows of the rain forest. Most macaws start out with gray or black eyes when young, which change to brown or yellow as they mature.

Red-fronted Macaw

Blue and Yellow Macaw

Blue and Gold Macaw

TEST EVERYTHING

Macaws are intelligent and curious birds. They use their strong, agile toes to grasp things, and they like to play with interesting objects they find. They will examine the objects from different angles, move them with their feet, test them with their tongues, and toss them around.

BEAKS THAT BREAK

Macaws have large, strong, curved beaks designed to crush nuts and seeds. A macaw's beak is so strong it can easily crush a whole Brazil nut—or a person's knuckle.

MAY I SEE THE MENU?

Macaws eat a variety of ripe and unripe fruits, nuts and seeds, flowers, leaves, stems, insects, and snails. Some species specialize in eating the hard fruits and nuts of palm trees.

Hyacinth Macaw

Bony Tongue
A macaw's tongue is dry, slightly scaly, and has a bone inside.

WHERE IN THE WORLD ARE MACAWS?

RANGE: Mexico and Central and South America

HABITAT: rain forests, forests along rivers, and grasslands with trees

Ibis

IBIS STUFF

TALLEST: giant ibis, 41 inches

SHORTEST: spot-breasted ibis, 18 inches

LIFE SPAN: to 25 years

NUMBER OF EGGS: 1 to 6

CONSERVATION STATUS: dwarf olive ibis, Waldrapp ibis, white-shouldered ibis, and giant ibis at critical risk

Southern Bald Ibis

COUNTING DOWN

Most ibises are fairly abundant but there are some species that are very rare and are in danger of becoming extinct. The dwindling populations are due to many factors including hunting, drainage of wetland feeding habitats, commercial logging of nesting trees, and pesticides.

In the Water, on the Land, or in the Air
Long legs and toes help make the ibis just as comfortable walking as flying or perching in trees.

Scarlet Ibis

Scarlet Ibis

DISAPPEARING BIRDS
There are now more Waldrapp ibises, also known as the hermit ibis or bald ibis, in zoos than in the wild. Only one wild flock is known to exist, found in North Africa and totaling only about 100 birds.

WHERE IN THE WORLD ARE IBISES?

RANGE: all continents except Antarctica

HABITAT: wetlands, forests, savannas, and coastal areas

Madagascar Crested Ibis

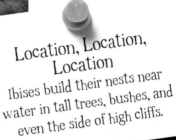

LOVE IS IN THE AIR

Ibises are normally silent birds, but during breeding season both males and females may make squeaks and breathing sounds described as *whoot-whoot*, *whoot-whooeeoh*, *yuk-pyuk-peuk-pek-peok*, or a wheezing *hnhh-hnhh*. Females also make a call that is similar to *whaank*, *turroh*, and *keerooh* when calling their young.

> **Location, Location, Location**
> Ibises build their nests near water in tall trees, bushes, and even the side of high cliffs.

Madagascar Crested Ibis Chick on Nest

Madagascar Crested Ibis

WHERE'S MY MUMMY?

The African sacred ibis was considered sacred in ancient Egypt but is no longer there. More than *one million* ibis mummies were found in Egypt.

Madagascar Crested Ibis Chick

"AH ONE, AH TWO . . ."

Ibises fly in flocks, either in a regular line or in a V formation. The whole flock will beat their wings in unison and even go from flapping to gliding at the same time.

TOP BILLING

The ibis uses its long, thin bill to probe water, mud, and cracks in dry ground for tasty grasshoppers, beetles, worms, crustaceans, fish, and carrion. Sensitive feelers on the inside of the bill help the bird identify the food without seeing it. Since the bird's nostrils are at the base of its bill, the ibis can still breathe while sticking its bill in the water or mud.

THE BLUSHING BIRD

The pink, orange, and red of scarlet ibises' feathers, legs, and feet come from the rich pigments in the algae and small crustaceans the birds eat. Adult birds have dark blue tips on four of their outer primary feathers.

Waldrapp Ibis

Waldrapp Ibis

Ostrich

OSTRICH STUFF

HEIGHT: male, 6.9 to 9 feet; female, 5.7 to 6.2 feet
WEIGHT: male, 220 to 287 pounds; female, 198 to 242 pounds
LIFE SPAN: 30 to 40 years
CONSERVATION STATUS: lower risk

WHAT ARE THE WINGS FOR?

Ostriches hold their wings out to help them balance when they run, especially if they suddenly change direction. Their wings also assist in body language: to show dominance, an ostrich holds its head up high and lifts its wings and tail feathers; to show submission, the head, wings, and tail droop down.

DO OSTRICHES BURY THEIR HEADS IN THE SAND?

Ostriches do not bury their heads in the sand. When an ostrich senses danger and cannot run away, it flops to the ground, remains still, and flattens its head on the ground in front of it. Because the head and neck are light in color, they blend in with the ground. From a distance, it looks like the ostrich has buried its head in the sand, because only the body is visible.

The Better to See You With

An ostrich's eye is almost two inches across, the largest eye of any land animal.

WHERE IN THE WORLD ARE OSTRICHES?

RANGE: central and southern Africa

HABITAT: savannas and deserts

BORN TO RUN

The ostrich is the largest and heaviest bird but is built for running. It has long, thick, and powerful legs and only two toes for greater speed. Ostriches sprint in short bursts up to 43 miles per hour, and they can maintain a steady speed of 31 miles per hour. Just one of an ostrich's strides can be up to 16 feet long.

HAVE A LUMP IN YOUR THROAT?

Ostriches eat whatever is available, mostly plants, roots, leaves, and seeds. They also munch on insects like locusts and small animals like lizards. When an ostrich eats, food is collected in the crop at the top of the throat until there is a large enough lump to slide down the neck.

STONE SOUP

Ostriches eat things that other animals can't digest. Their intestines are 46 feet long to absorb as many nutrients as possible. These big birds also swallow sand, pebbles, and small stones that help grind up food in their gizzard.

Long Toenails
Ostriches have a four-inch claw on each foot, and their kick is powerful enough to kill a lion.

Female and Male South African Ostriches with Chicks

WILL YOU BE MY VALENTINE?

During courtship, the black-and-white male ostrich uses his dramatic coloring to attract the light brown female. He sinks slowly to the ground, almost like he's bowing, and begins to wave and shake the feathers of first one wing and then the other while moving his tail up and down. He then gets up and moves toward the female, holding his wings out and stamping to impress her.

A BIG BIRD HERD

Ostriches sometimes live in large groups of 100 or more, but most groups are usually about 10 birds, or even just a male and female. The groups have a pecking order, with a head male that establishes and defends a territory, an alpha female, and several other females.

Two Dozen Eggs in a Shell
One ostrich egg is equivalent to the weight of about 24 chicken eggs.

NESTING DUTY

The alpha hen shares the task of hatching the eggs and caring for the chicks with the male. The alpha hen lays her eggs in the center of the nest to make sure they have the best chance of hatching; then the other hens lay their eggs in the same nest. The alpha hen is on duty during the day, then the male takes over and sits on the nest at night. A few days after the chicks hatch, they leave the nest but stay with their parents. The adults shelter them under their wings to protect them from sun and rain, and they defend the chicks against predators.

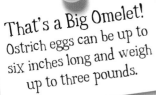

That's a Big Omelet!
Ostrich eggs can be up to six inches long and weigh up to three pounds.

BIG SHAGGY BIRD

Ostrich feathers are loose, soft, and smooth. They don't hook together the way feathers of other birds do, giving ostriches that "shaggy" look. The feathers can also get soaked in a rainstorm, because ostriches do not have the special gland many birds have to waterproof their feathers while preening.

Owl

Eurasian Eagle-owl

American Great Gray Owl

Spectacled Owl

IT'S TOUGH BEING A VOLE

Owls compete with each other for territory and food; but, fortunately, owls of different species can coexist by hunting at different times of the day or night. The great gray owl, the Ural owl, and the tawny owl all live in the same range; but the great gray owl is unique among owls in that it is a daytime hunter. It prefers voles as prey. The tawny owl also hunts voles, but only at night; and the Ural owl hunts larger prey, such as squirrels.

WHERE IN THE WORLD ARE OWLS?

RANGE: every continent except Antarctica

HABITAT: all habitats

Shhh ... Mouse Alert
An owl can hear a mouse stepping on a twig 75 feet away. This is because they have two huge ears that are incredibly sharp.

NIGHT FLIGHT

Owls fly at night, and they fly low to the ground as they look for small rodents. Larger owls have been known to carry off young deer, weasels, and foxes.

Western Burrowing Owl

Great Horned Owl

STEALTH BOMBER

Owls are silent in flight. Where other birds have stiff feathers that make a whooshing sound when they fly, owl feathers have soft edges that allow them to fly silently. This allows owls to swoop down on prey without being heard.

Covered Legs and Feet
Many owl species have a thick covering of feathers on their legs and feet, which protects them from snake and rat bites.

Western Burrowing Owl

BABY, IT'S COLD OUTSIDE
Snowy owls live in the Arctic, where the cold tundra is home. Thick, warm feathers cover even their bills and toes, and provide effective insulation against roaring winds and freezing temperatures.

No Place to Hide
Owls have the best night vision of any animal and their hearing is excellent.

Eurasian Eagle-owl

NIGHT VISION
Owls have eyes so big that they cannot move them. An owl must move its entire head to follow the movement of prey; but this gives the owl better focus, since both eyes are looking in the same direction. Although it seems that an owl can twist its head completely around, most owls actually turn their heads no more than 270 degrees in either direction.

Barn Owl

PRIVILEGED CHILDHOOD

Young owl chicks get the best of care from their mother for about three months. They are fed, protected from predators, and learn to fly and hunt so they can leave the nest and find territories of their own. Fathers are also often involved in rearing the chicks, including sitting on the eggs and bringing food back for the family.

Thailand Bay Owl Chicks

Burrowing Owl Chicks

CAN I TRUST YOU?

Before owls can begin courting, they must first overcome a natural fear of one another. Male owls bring offerings of food and drop it near the female.

Owl Hole
Most owls live in trees, but burrowing owls live in underground burrows.

TO EVERY PURPOSE THERE IS AN OWL

Owls live everywhere. Some owls prefer cold climates, while others live in deserts or rain forests. Some, like barn owls, hunt in wide open spaces. Others, like long-eared owls, make their home in the forest. A small wingspan on a chestnut-backed owl helps it navigate around trees in a tropical rain forest, while the longer wings on a barn owl are ideal for cruising over open fields.

THE EARLY BIRD GETS THE WORM

The number of eggs an owl lays depends upon the food supply. If food is scarce, only two or three eggs are laid; if food is available, six or more eggs are laid. Chicks hatch two days apart. The oldest chicks get the most food.

Stork

STORK STUFF

TALLEST: marabou stork, 4.9 feet
SHORTEST: hammerkop, 2 feet
LONGEST WINGSPAN: marabou stork, 10.5 feet
HEAVIEST: marabou stork, 19.6 pounds
LIGHTEST: hammerkop, 16.1 ounces
LIFE SPAN: about 30 years
NUMBER OF EGGS: 2 to 5
CONSERVATION STATUS: Oriental white stork, Storm's stork, and greater adjutant stork endangered; most stork species vulnerable

Saddlebill Stork

Marabou Stork

Maguari Stork

OH BABY, BABY

When stork chicks hatch, they are almost naked, but they quickly develop fluffy down feathers. Their parents bring them food, and the chicks eat up to 60 percent of their own body weight per day. After about three or four weeks, the chicks stand up in the nest and flap their stubby wings. After a few months, their flight feathers grow in and they learn to fly. Even then, they depend on their parents for food for several more weeks.

WHERE IN THE WORLD ARE STORKS?

RANGE: all continents except Antarctica; most common in tropical regions

HABITAT: wetlands, grasslands, tropical forests, and savannas

Storm's Stork Chicks

Hammerkop Stork Nest

The hammerkop
stork builds a dome
on its nest, which
can be as big as six
feet around and
weigh more than
100 pounds.

Storm's Stork Nest

HOME SWEET NEST

Most storks build their nests in trees. Some build
a new nest each year, while others use the same
nest again and again, adding sticks and twigs until
the nest is huge. Stork nests can be more than
nine feet deep and six feet wide. Small birds like
sparrows, starlings, and wrens sometimes built
their nest between the sticks of the storks' nests.

Oriental or Eastern White Stork

Eastern Hammerkop Stork

NESTING PARTY

At nesting time, some storks live in large
groups of as many as several thousand birds.
During courtship, storks do a lot of bill
clacking—rattling the two halves of their bills
together, making the group very loud.

Adjutant (Lesser) Stork

Yellow-billed Stork

African Openbill Stork

WHAT'S FOR DINNER?

Storks can wade into deep water in search of food. They stretch out their longs necks and pluck dinner from the reeds or grasses.

African Openbill Stork

Yellow-billed Stork

CATCH OF THE DAY

Most storks live in wetlands or near water and eat fish, amphibians, small reptiles, shellfish, and insects. Some storks eat small mammals like rodents and moles.

Yellow-billed Stork

I'D RATHER BE FLYING

Storks fly by soaring on warm air currents, only occasionally flapping their long, broad wings. They stretch their necks out and dangle their legs behind them as they fly.

Wood Stork

SWING YOUR BEAK

A marabou stork's bill grows all its life and can be 13.6 inches long. These storks use their large, heavy bill as a weapon.

Marabou Stork

DELIVERING THE BABY

The legend of storks bringing babies probably began in Europe where the white stork nests on the chimneys of houses. To have a stork nest on your chimney is considered good luck.

TAKEOUT FOR DINNER

Wood storks and milky storks feed in murky waters and have sensitive bills. They stand still with their bills in the water; and when they feel dinner passing by, they gobble it up. Shoebill storks watch for fish to surface and spear them with their sharp bills.

Storm's Stork

Pelican

PELICAN STUFF

LENGTH: 4 to 6 feet
WINGSPAN: 6 to 11 feet
WEIGHT: 10 to 17 pounds
LIFE SPAN: to 30 years
NUMBER OF EGGS: 1 to 3
CONSERVATION STATUS: Dalmatian pelican and spot-billed pelican vulnerable

Great White Pelican

Dalmatian Pelican

WHERE IN THE WORLD ARE PELICANS?

RANGE: every continent except for Antarctica

HABITAT: temperate and tropical shores; certain species found along seacoasts, and other species near inland lakes

American White Pelican

DIVE BOMB FISHERMAN

The brown pelican sights fish when flying up to 70 feet over water, then dives in headfirst. It may submerge completely or only partially, depending on the height of the dive. Air sacs under its skin cushion the impact of hitting the water and also help the bird bob back to the surface like a feathered cork.

UNIQUE FEET

The pelican is short-legged with a big body. They are strong swimmers and their webbed feet push through the water. Pelicans and their relatives, such as cormorants, gannets, and boobies, are the only birds with a totipalmate foot. This means that webbing connects all four of their toes, even the back toe.

Pink-backed Pelican

"A WONDERFUL BIRD IS THE PELICAN, HIS BILL WILL HOLD MORE THAN HIS BELICAN. . . ." The lower half of a pelican's bill can hold up to three gallons of water, which is two to three times more than can be held in its stomach. The old rhyme is true!

MULTI-USE POUCH

Pelicans are one of the only birds with a pouch under the bill. This enormous, naked skin pouch hangs from the lower half of the pelican's long, straight bill, which is hooked at the tip. The pouch is used to catch fish but is also helpful in warm weather. While roosting in the hot sun, pelicans can open their bills and flap their pouch as a fan to cool off.

Pink-backed Pelican

GRACEFUL ONLY IN FLIGHT

Pelicans are splendid fliers and with their giant wings can soar like eagles. Pelicans fly in flocks, sometimes in a V formation, but usually in a single line. Getting up in the air, however, can be challenging without the help of the wind. Pelicans must run over the water, beat their big wings, and pound the surface of the water with both feet in unison to get enough speed for takeoff.

WORK SMART, NOT HARD

In the Prespa Lakes of Greece, the Dalmatian pelican flies with cormorants. The cormorants dive deep into the water, which brings the fish to the surface and the pelican scoops them up.

Southern White Pelican

American White Pelicans

WHAT'S FOR DINNER?

Pelicans mainly eat fish, but if a small reptile or amphibian comes their way, they will eat that too. Pelicans use their pouch like a fishing net to scoop the fish into their bill then tip their head forward to drain the water. They do not carry fish very far in their pouch but swallow them soon after catching them.

NEVER ON A DIET

It is a good thing pelicans are successful fishers because they are among the largest of all birds. An adult pelican may eat up to four pounds of fish each day! Around the world, pelicans have been accused of competing with fishermen as well as with the commercial fishing industry. Numerous studies, however, have shown that pelicans usually eat fish, such as carp, shiners, mullet, and minnows, which are not commercial fish.

Southern White Pelican

Pink-backed Pelican

Super-Size Me
There is one documented case of a 30-pound pelican!

SHORE FISHING

Pink-backed pelicans and spot-billed pelicans are quick grabbers. These pelicans paddle along in the water, usually where there is a lot of vegetation where they can hide. They slowly swim up to prey and then catch it with a quick lunge. These birds hunt alone.

Adult Pink-backed Pelican and Chick

PELICAN SCHOOL OF FISHING

The American white pelican is a group fisher. Four to five American white pelicans swim side by side and glide in a semicircle facing the shore. Then, with much wing flapping and water splashing, they drive the fish toward the shore. Once the fish are in shallow water, the pelicans scoop them up in their bills.

Like Peas in a Pod
A group of pelicans is called a pod.

Pod of American White Pelicans

Pod of Dalmatian Pelicans

Pink-backed Pelican Chicks on Nest with Parent

BIRDS OF A FEATHER FLOCK TOGETHER

Pelicans live in flocks with the young and adults of both sexes grouping together throughout much of the year. They nest in colonies in trees, bushes, or on the ground.

PARENTING PELICANS

Pelicans nest in large colonies, either near the water or in trees, depending on the species and habitat. During breeding season, both males and females use their pouches to carry nest-building materials: twigs, grass, and feathers. The parents take turns incubating the eggs. The eggs hatch a day apart, and the first chick to hatch often attacks its younger siblings so it gets the most food. The young are not fed from the pouch; instead, the parents open their mouths wide and the young reach down into their gullets for food.

Pink-backed Pelican

Kingfisher

KINGFISHER STUFF

LARGEST: laughing kookaburra, to 18 inches
SMALLEST: African dwarf kingfisher, 3.9 inches
HEAVIEST: laughing kookaburra, to 17 ounces
LIGHTEST: African dwarf kingfisher, .03 to 0.4 ounces
LIFE SPAN: to 15 years
NUMBER OF EGGS: 2 to 10
CONSERVATION STATUS: Marquesas kingfisher and the Micronesian kingfisher endangered; 7 species vulnerable

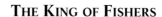
Micronesian Kingfisher Chick

THE KING OF FISHERS

Kingfishers eat fish and are very good at catching it. They perch above a stream, river, or lake and wait for a fish to swim into view. The bird dives down to snatch up the fish then returns to its perch to prepare its meal. The kingfisher beats the fish against the perch to break the bones for easier swallowing. The bird then juggles the fish in its beak and swallows it head first, to avoid getting scraped by the scales on the way down.

BRIGHT AND FAST

Kingfishers are known for their looks: stocky bodies, long, thick bills, and striking colors and markings. Many species are decked out in feathers of bright blue, green, turquoise, red, or gold. Some have splotches, dashes, stripes, or speckles.

Micronesian Kingfisher Chick

WHERE IN THE WORLD ARE KINGFISHERS?

RANGE: Asia, Africa, Australia, and South America; some species in Europe and North America

HABITAT: along banks of rivers and lakes; forests and open woodlands; along seashores or in deserts

BUILT TOUGH

Most kingfishers have short legs and strong feet, since they spend most of their time perched on a stalk, twig, or branch while keeping an eye out for a meal. Even though they are chunky birds, kingfishers can fly fast. Some, like the pied kingfisher, can even flap their wings fast enough to hover over water.

WHAT'S FOR DINNER?

Even kingfishers that eat mostly fish also eat other things on occasion, like crabs, crayfish, snails, and frogs. Kingfishers that live in forests, grasslands, and deserts have a different diet, dining on a variety of insects, spiders, reptiles, and small mammals, which they catch by spying the prey from a perch and darting out to snap it up.

Open Wide!
The Amazon kingfisher has a bill about 2.8 inches long but can eat a fish that is 6.7 inches long!

White-breasted Kingfisher

Woodland Kingfisher

SNAKE FOR LUNCH AND DINNER

The blue-winged kookaburra is known as a snake hunter. It grabs a snake behind the head and bashes it against a branch or rock to kill it. Swallowing it is a bit trickier: the snake goes down head first, but the rest of the body hangs out of the kookaburra's mouth while it is digested bit by bit!

Pygmy Kingfisher

Stay Away!
Sacred kingfishers are aggressive and fearless in defending their nests. They have been known to attack weasels, cats, dogs, and other birds that come too close.

White-breasted Kingfisher Chick

KNIFE SHARPENER

The kingfisher's dagger-shaped bill often seems too long or too big for the rest of the bird, but it is well designed for capturing food. Kingfishers keep their impressive bills clean by scraping them against a branch, first one side, then the other, until they are satisfied that the bill is in good condition.

ICE BREAKER

When a common kingfisher dives after a fish, it can completely submerge in the water and fold its wings backward to create a V shape. It can even dive straight through a layer of thin ice to catch a fish below!

KINGFISHER LANGUAGE

Kingfishers use a variety of calls to announce their territory, warn off other birds, and communicate with a mate and their chicks. They shriek, scream, click, whistle, chuckle, rattle, and chirp.

CLEANLINESS IS NEXT TO GODLINESS

Kingfishers keep clean and bathe by diving into water then perching in the sun to dry and preen their feathers. Some use their wings to scrub and scratch the tops of their heads.

Alarm Clock
An Australian Aborigine legend says that the gods chose the kookaburra to wake people and animals at the beginning of each day.

Blue-breasted Kingfisher

THE LAUGHING BIRD

The most famous bird call is probably that of the laughing kookaburra's, a *kooa haha haha* that sounds like someone laughing. You might have heard this sound used in movies set in the jungles of Africa or South America—although the kookaburra is really only native to Australia!

Kookaburra

MOVING TOWARD THE DOOR

Once the chicks are hatched, the parents bring food all the way into the nesting chamber. As the chicks grow, they start to move toward the burrow's entrance to meet the adults. Eventually, they perch at the entrance or even on a branch nearby, waiting to be fed. After fledging (growing their flight feathers and learning to fly), it can be a few days to a few weeks before the chicks start finding and catching their own food.

HUNGRY? CRY UNCLE

Most kingfisher species are solitary, only pairing up with a mate during breeding season. But laughing and blue-winged kookaburras live in family groups made up of a male and female pair and their older offspring, which help raise the new chicks. These helpers are mostly males instead of females.

Micronesian Kingfisher Chick

Micronesian Kingfisher

Male Micronesian Kingfisher

Kingfisher Nest Box

DIGGING IN

Kingfishers don't build nests of sticks or plants. Instead, they nest in burrows that they dig into dirt banks, tree cavities, or old termite mounds. A male and female pair works together to create the burrow, taking turns digging out the soil with their feet. The burrow takes about three to seven days to complete. It often slopes upward to avoid flooding and is usually about three to six and a half feet long, although the record is a 28-foot burrow dug by a pair of giant kingfishers. The burrow ends in a nesting chamber that is about eight to 12 inches wide and six to seven inches high. This is where the eggs are laid and the chicks raised.

Mother and Baby Pygmy Chimpanzees

Mammals

WHAT IN THE WORLD ARE MAMMALS?

- regulate temperature (are endotherms)
- vertebrates (have a backbone)
- have hair on their bodies
- produce milk
- usually give birth to live babies

MAMMAL STUFF

LARGEST: blue whale, 100 feet

HEAVIEST: blue whale, 300,000 pounds (150 tons)

LARGEST LAND MAMMAL: male African elephant, shoulder height 10.5 feet

HEAVIEST LAND MAMMAL: male African elephant, 15,000 pounds (7.5 tons)

SMALLEST: Kitti's hog-nosed bat, 6-inch wingspan

LIGHTEST: Kitti's hog-nosed bat, 0.053 ounces

FASTEST: cheetah, 70 miles per hour

NUMBER OF SPECIES: more than 4,000 known

Bactrian Camel

THREE CLASSES OF MAMMALS

Placental. Babies are born developed and can live outside of their mothers' bodies. Humans are placental mammals.

Marsupial. Babies are helpless when born; they crawl into a pouch on Mom's belly and nurse there until big enough to live outside. Koalas and kangaroos are marsupials.

Monotreme. Babies are hatched from leathery eggs, then cling to the mother's fur and suck milk through her pores. Duck-billed platypus is a monotreme.

African Elephant

Gorilla

Male Gorilla

Male Gorilla

KNUCKLE-WALKERS

Gorillas stand upright, but they prefer to walk using their hands as well as their legs. Their arms are much longer than their legs, and they can use the backs of their fingers like extra feet when they walk. Gorillas and chimpanzees are the only animals able to knuckle walk.

GENTLE GIANTS

Gorillas are the largest of all primates—the group of animals that includes monkeys, lemurs, orangutans, chimpanzees, and humans. Gorillas are peaceful, family-oriented, plant-eating animals.

SEE-FOOD DIET

Almost everything a gorilla eats is plant material, so life in the forest is like living in a huge restaurant. Gorilla food includes leaves, stems, fruits, seeds, and roots. And gorillas love to eat—it's their favorite activity! An adult male will eat up to 40 pounds of food each day. Gorillas' large stomachs can hold the bulky food they eat. Strong jaws help them chew tough stems.

Troop of Gorillas

EVERY DAY IS MOVING DAY

A gorilla troop doesn't stay in the same place for more than a day. Each morning the silverback leads his troop to a new area where food is plentiful. After a morning of munching, adult gorillas gather leaves, twigs, and branches to make a day nest for resting while the youngsters play. After their nap, the gorillas will eat again until bedtime, when they make yet another nest, either on the ground or in a tree, for a good night's sleep. Gorillas never use the same nest twice.

Hair This!
Gorillas are very hairy, but not on their faces, palms, and soles of their feet.

TROOP LEADER

A group of gorillas living together is called a troop. There can be five to 30 gorillas in a troop, led by a strong, experienced male known as a silverback. He is responsible for the safety and well-being of the members of his troop. The silverback makes all the decisions, such as where the troop will travel for food each day, when they will stop to eat or rest, and where they will spend the night.

Sometimes a young male from another troop will challenge the silverback. The silverback will beat his chest with cupped hands, scream, bare his teeth, then charge forward. Sometimes he will break off branches and shake them at the intruder.

I Nose You!
No two gorilla noses are alike! Researchers in the wild take close-up photos of each gorilla's face to help identify individuals.

WHERE IN THE WORLD ARE GORILLAS?

RANGE: African continent, mainly along the equator

HABITAT: tropical rain forests, mountain slopes, and bamboo forests

Baby Lowland Gorilla

BABY BUSINESS

A female gorilla will have babies when she is about eight years old. At five to six months old, a baby learns to walk; and by 18 months of age, it can follow Mom on foot for short distances. The safest place for the youngster, however, is its mother's back.

Mother and Three-month-old Baby

Pygmy Chimpanzee

CHIMPANZEE STUFF

LENGTH: to 3 feet
WEIGHT: to 110 pounds in the wild, to 135 pounds in captivity
LIFE SPAN: about 50 years
NUMBER OF YOUNG AT BIRTH: 1 to 2
SIZE AT BIRTH: 2.8 pounds
CONSERVATION STATUS: endangered

AROUND THE NEIGHBORHOOD

Chimpanzees live in a community of family groups. Each group contains about six to 10 individuals. An entire chimp community can sometimes have as many as 100 members, made up of many different family groups.

Grin and Scare It
Chimpanzees make a grunting sound when they are happy. A toothy grin actually indicates fear or anxiety.

TAKE A GOOD LOOK

There is no hair on a chimpanzee's face, hands, or feet, but the rest of its body is covered with either long black or brown hair. Chimps don't have tails. But they do have large ears that stick out a bit, which helps them hear other chimps in a dense forest. Chimps have opposable thumbs to help them grasp branches and they have fingernails and toenails.

WHERE IN THE WORLD ARE PYGMY CHIMPANZEES?

RANGE: northern and central Democratic Republic of Congo

HABITAT: tropical rain forests

Two-month-old Baby

OH BABY, BABY

A newborn chimp is extremely helpless. Soon after birth, the baby learns to cling to its mother's underside. Later it will transfer to her back and ride piggyback for the next seven months or so. Young chimps get milk from their mothers until they are about three years old. They begin walking on their own at about age four, but stay with their mothers for a few more years, learning the skills they need to survive.

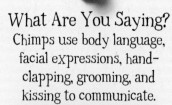

What Are You Saying?
Chimps use body language, facial expressions, hand-clapping, grooming, and kissing to communicate.

KNUCKLE-WALKERS

Chimpanzees, like gorillas and orangutans, are great apes. They walk on the soles of their feet and the knuckles of their hands. This way of walking has earned them the title of knuckle-walkers.

Flying Chimp
A chimp named Ham orbited Earth in 1961 and was taught simple commands to help test space travel for human astronauts. Ham became the first "American" in space!

DINNER IS SERVED

Chimpanzees eat seeds, fruit, leaves, bark, honey, flowers, and insects. Chimpanzees use tools to help them gather food. They use a branch to poke into an ant or termite hill to get the insects inside. When water is scarce, chimps chew leaves until they are soft and sponge-like and then use them to soak up rainwater from the inside of trees.

Mother and Baby

Orangutan

Female Orangutan

DAYDREAMERS

Orangutans are the loners and the daydreamers of the great apes. While chimps and gorillas are usually found in groups called troops, orangutans are more solitary. Other apes might go from tree to tree searching for fruit, but an orang will just sit in the forest canopy for hours on end until the location of the hidden fruit seems to mysteriously reveal itself. Then it will swing over for its meal. Orangs have even been known to watch villagers use boats to cross the local waterways, and then untie a boat and ride it across the river on their own.

RELAXED PROBLEM SOLVERS

Scientists like to explain the orangutan's unique approach to problem solving with this example: If a chimp is given an oddly shaped peg and several different holes to try to put it in, the chimp will immediately try shoving the peg in various holes until it finds the hole that the peg fits in. But an orang will stare off into space, or even scratch itself with the peg. Then, after a while, it will offhandedly stick the peg into the correct hole while looking at something else that has caught its interest.

WHERE IN THE WORLD ARE ORANGUTANS?

RANGE: northern Sumatra and parts of Borneo

HABITAT: rain forests

All Arms
Orangutan arms stretch out longer than their bodies— over seven feet from fingertip to fingertip!

Male Orangutan

CHEEK TO CHEEK
When they are about 15 years old, male orangs develop large cheek pads. Female orangs find these pads very attractive. When males are fighting, they charge at each other and break branches. And if that doesn't scare one of them away, they grab and bite each other on the cheek pads or ears until one of them gives up and runs away.

TREE HOUSE
Orangutans spend most of their lives in trees and travel by swinging from branch to branch with their long arms. They usually build a new nest every night, but occasionally reuse one. They use leafy branches to shelter themselves from rain and sun and even drape large leaves over themselves like a poncho.

Mother and Baby

Eight-month-old Orangutan

IT'S YOU AND ME, MOM
Orangutans have the longest childhood of the great apes. Young orangs usually stay with their mothers until they're about eight years old or older. The solitary animals must learn all the lessons of finding fruit, building night nests, and other survival techniques before they set off on their own.

Monkeys

MONKEY STUFF

LARGEST: baboon, to 3.6 feet

SMALLEST: pygmy marmoset, 4.6 to 5.9 inches

HEAVIEST: baboon, to 80 pounds

LIGHTEST: pygmy marmoset, 3 to 4.9 ounces

LOUDEST: howler monkeys—their howls can be heard almost 2 miles through the forest and more than 3 miles over open areas

FASTEST: Patas monkeys, up to 31 miles per hour on the ground

LIFE SPAN: 10 to 50 years

CONSERVATION STATUS: many species at critical risk including southern muriqui, black-faced lion tamarin, and Tonkin snub-nosed monkey

Angolan Black-and-white Colobus Monkey

Pygmy Marmoset

MONKEYING AROUND

All monkeys can use their hands and feet for holding on to branches, but some monkeys can use their tails too. Tails that can grab and hold are called prehensile. These special tails are ridged on the underside and very flexible, so that they can grab a tree branch or pick up something as small as a peanut! Prehensile tails come in handy for holding on while the monkey collects food: flowers, fruits, nuts, leaves, seeds, insects, birds' eggs, spiders, and small mammals.

Brown Spider Monkey

WHERE IN THE WORLD ARE MONKEYS?

OLD WORLD MONKEYS

RANGE: Africa, central to southern Asia, Japan, and India

HABITAT: rain forests, islands, steppes, mountains, and savannas

NEW WORLD MONKEYS

RANGE: Mexico, Central and South America

HABITAT: tropical rain forests

Golden-bellied Mangabey

Geoffroy's Marmoset

Baboon

Patas Monkey

Howler Monkey

Monkey Hot Tub
Japanese macaques live in parts of Japan where it snows. These monkeys find hot springs and spend much of the winter soaking in the warm water.

READ MY LIPS

Monkeys get their message across through sounds, facial expressions, and body movements. To monkeys, staring is a threat, so they look down or away to avoid threatening other monkeys. Loud vocalizations can mean, "Stay out. This is my territory." Grinning or pulling the lip up to show the teeth is a sign of aggression or anger, because biting is one way monkeys fight and defend themselves. Other signs of aggression include head bobbing, yawning, and jerking the head and shoulders forward.

Schmidt's Spot-nosed Monkey

Gone Fishing
Some monkeys can swim. They may swim across a stream or river to avoid predators or get to food. Allen's swamp monkeys lay leaves on top of the water, then grab the fish that hide underneath.

PICK MY NITS

Monkeys express affection and make peace by grooming each other. Grooming helps monkeys keep their fur clean of dirt, dead skin, and parasites, but it also helps them build and maintain good social relationships.

PARDON ME!

Among leaf-eating colobus monkeys, like the Angolan black-and-white colobus, burping is a friendly social gesture. Their four-chambered stomachs digest leaves by a process of bacterial fermentation, which produces lots of gas.

WEIGHT: 17 to 28 pounds
LIFE SPAN: 25 to 30 years
NUMBER OF YOUNG AT BIRTH: usually 1
WEIGHT AT BIRTH: about 6 ounces
CONSERVATION STATUS: endangered

What's for Lunch?
About half of the siamang's diet consists of leaves. The other half is fruits, flowers, buds, and insects for crunch!

UNTIL DEATH DO US PART
Siamang pairs usually stay together for life. Paired males and females sing duets and create a unique song. A siamang family consists of one adult male, one adult female, and two or three immature offspring.

CAN YOU HEAR ME NOW?
Siamang calls include booms and barks, made louder by an inflatable throat sac. These calls can be heard up to two miles away. The calls are used primarily for claiming territory, which can be as large as 50 acres. First thing in the morning, a family's adult female will start a territorial hooting that the others join, and the noisy warning to other siamangs can last 30 minutes.

WHERE IN THE WORLD ARE SIAMANGS?

RANGE: Malaysia and Indonesia

HABITAT: rain forests and monsoon forests

SHARE AND SHARE ALIKE
The siamang is the largest of the 14 species of gibbons. They can share territory with other gibbons because the siamangs are largely leaf eaters and do not compete for the forest fruit.

HANDS AND FEET
Siamangs have four long fingers and a smaller opposable thumb on each hand. Their feet have five toes, and their big toe is opposable. Siamangs can grasp and carry things with both their hands and their feet.

EARLY TO BED
At around 4:00 to 6:00 PM, the group settles into a sleeping tree for the night. A family of siamangs likes to stick together as they go about their daily business. During activities, group members are only about 30 feet apart.

WHAT DO I DO WITH MY ARMS?
Siamangs don't have tails, but they have arms longer than their legs. The siamang's arm span is 4.9 feet and they can cover up to 10 feet in a single swing. When not swinging through trees, they walk along the branches with outstretched arms for balance. When they walk on the ground, they hold their arms over their heads.

OH BABY, BABY
Baby siamangs are born hairless except for a small tuft of hair on top of their heads. Soon after the baby is born, it holds onto its mother's fur and clings to her belly. The father does his share of raising the baby and takes over the daily care of the youngster when it is about one year old. The youngster is weaned early in its second year. Young siamangs stay with their families for five to seven years then venture out to start their own family groups.

Mandrill

MANDRILL STUFF

LENGTH: male, to 32 inches; female, to 22 inches
TAIL LENGTH: 2 to 3 inches
WEIGHT: male, 55 pounds; female, 25 pounds
LIFE SPAN: to 40 years
NUMBER OF YOUNG AT BIRTH: 1 to 2
WEIGHT AT BIRTH: 1 to 2 pounds
CONSERVATION STATUS: endangered

Male Mandrill

BIG AND BRILLIANT

Mandrills are one of the largest species of monkey in the world. Their furry head crests, manes, and beards are quite impressive, but what really gets attention is their bright color. They have thick ridges along their noses that are purple and blue; their noses and lips are red and beards, golden.

WHERE IN THE WORLD ARE MANDRILLS?

RANGE: equatorial region of western Africa

HABITAT: primarily rain forests

LET'S DO TAKE-OUT

Mandrills have large cheek pouches inside their mouths that they stuff full of food to eat at a safer location. Mandrills spend most of their time on the ground foraging for seeds, nuts, fruits, and small animals.

Mother and Baby

Grin and Bare It
Mandrills shake their heads and "grin" widely to show their canine teeth, which can be over two inches long. This is a friendly gesture among mandrills.

OH BABY, BABY
Female mandrills usually give birth to one baby. The infant is born with a dark fur coat and can cling to its mother's belly immediately. At two months of age it starts to lose its baby hair and its adult coat comes in.

FAMILY LIFE
Mandrills live in troops of about 20. The dominant male is the leader and has the boldest, brightest colors. Super troops of several hundred mandrills may gather when food is readily available. The troop sleeps in a different tree each night.

Female Mandrill

Male Mandrill

Canadian Lynx

ROUGH TONGUE

Cat tongues are rough because they are covered with rows of rough bumps called papillae, which scrape hair off hides and meat off bones. The papillae also help hold water on the tongue when the cat drinks.

DID YOU HEAR THAT?

A cat's ears are controlled by more than 20 muscles, and the ears move independently of each other. One can point forward while the other points back. A cat's ears can turn in all directions, including behind the cat, to catch sounds. Some small cats, like the North American lynx, have extra-long tufts of fur on the tops of their ears. The tufts are sensitive to sound waves, helping the cat pinpoint the location of a sound.

Cougar/Puma/Mountain Lion

Ocelot

More Than a Feeling

Cats have sensitive whiskers, called vibrissae, on their lips, cheeks, chins, eyebrows, and forelegs that give them information about their environment. The whiskers are deeply embedded in the skin and connected to nerve endings that transmit information to the brain, so a cat can feel its way as it moves.

Clouded Leopard

The Better to See You With

Cats have a layer of tissue in their eyes called the tapetum lucidum, which bounces light back through the retina a second time and increases the amount of light by which the cat has to see. That's what causes the "eyeshine" that you see with cats at night.

Clouded Leopard

Small Cat or Big Cat?

Scientists divide all cats into small cats or big cats. But this distinction is not based on size.

Big Cats	Small Cats
• Roar	• Mew, scream, growl
• Purr only when breathing out	• Purr nonstop
• Pupils close to a circle	• Pupils close to a vertical slit
• Nose has fur directly above the wet tip	• Nose has a leathery strip across the top directly above the wet tip

WHERE IN THE WORLD ARE CATS?

RANGE: all parts of the world except Australia and Antarctica

HABITAT: all habitats

Black-footed Cat

Mountain Lion

Mountain Lion Stuff

LENGTH: males, 3 to 6 feet; females, 3 to 5 feet
SHOULDER HEIGHT: 1.9 to 2.3 feet
WEIGHT: males, 147 to 227 pounds; females, 79 to 132 pounds
LIFE SPAN: to 20 years
NUMBER OF YOUNG AT BIRTH: 1 to 6, usually 3 to 4
SIZE AT BIRTH: 8 to 15 ounces
CONSERVATION STATUS: common in many areas; some subspecies vulnerable or endangered

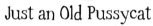

Just an Old Pussycat
Even though we hear it a lot in movies and on TV, mountain lions don't make that wildcat scream very often. More common vocalizations are whistles, squeaks, growls, purrs, hisses, and yowls.

WHAT WAS YOUR NAME AGAIN?
Mountain lion, puma, cougar, panther—it's still the same cat, the largest of the small cat species. Because this cat has such a large range, people from different regions call it by different names.

WHERE IN THE WORLD ARE MOUNTAIN LIONS?

RANGE: western Canada, western United States and Florida, Central America, South America

HABITAT: forests, swamps, and grasslands

HOME ON THE RANGE

Mountain lions live in areas called "home ranges," which vary in size from 30 to 125 square miles. To rest or escape from bad weather, mountain lions find shelter in thick brush, rocky crevices, or caves. Only mothers set up a specific den, where they give birth to their cubs and stay with them until they are old enough to go hunting at about six months.

Mother and Cub at Den Entrance (Superstock)

Mountain Lion Cub (Superstock)

GETTING A JUMP ON DINNER

Mountain lions have large paws with sharp claws. Their hind legs are large and muscular and give them great jumping power. Mountain lions can jump 18 feet from the ground into a tree. They have been known to jump 20 feet up or down a hillside. That's the height of many two-story buildings.

Run, Cougar, Run

Mountain lions can run fast and have a flexible spine that helps them maneuver around obstacles and change direction quickly.

(Superstock)

IT ALL TASTES GOOD WHEN YOU'RE HUNGRY

Mountain lions eat a variety of prey, depending on where they live, including deer, pigs, raccoons, armadillos, hares, and squirrels. Some larger cats even bring down animals as big as an elk or a moose. Some mountain lions eat porcupines—quills and all!

(Superstock)

LLLST: male Sumatran tiger, 10 feet

HEAVIEST: male Siberian tiger, 400 pounds and up

LIFE SPAN: 15 to 20 years

NUMBER OF YOUNG AT BIRTH: 1 to 7, usually 2 to 3

SIZE AT BIRTH: 2.2 pounds

CONSERVATION STATUS: endangered

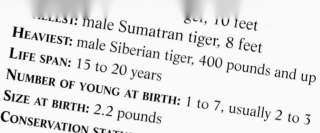

Sumatran Tiger

Malaysian Tiger

HUNTING GEAR

Tigers' front paws are large with five toes on each. The tiger pulls his claws inside while he walks, which keeps them sharp. Tigers mark their territory by scratching on trees. This also sharpens the claws.

Bengal Tiger

BLACK AND WHITE AND ORANGE ALL OVER

Tigers are recognized by their orange, black, and white striped coat which is good camouflage in the long grass. Dark stripes on a pale background break up the tiger's outline as it lies in wait for prey. Tigers can also be black with tan stripes, all white (albino), or white and tan. The "white tigers" found in some zoos are not albino, but rather the white-and-tan color variation with blue eyes. (True albinos have pink eyes.)

Sumatran Tiger

Bengal Tiger

Malaysian Tiger

GO JUMP IN A LAKE

Some cats do like water—and tigers are among them. On a hot, steamy day in the Asian forest, tigers will take to the river to cool off. In colder climates, they enjoy the snow.

LOVIN' THOSE LEFTOVERS

Tigers like pigs and deer for dinner, while in some parts of Asia they may bring down a rhino or elephant calf. A tiger quietly stalks its prey for 20 or 30 minutes. Then it grabs its prey by the neck with large canine teeth and powerful jaws. A tiger kills once or twice a week. After it stuffs itself, it covers the leftovers with grass and dirt. The tiger keeps coming back for the next few days for small snacks.

No Fake I.D.s
Each tiger has its very own stripe pattern. Researchers who observe tigers can identify individuals by their unique stripes.

TIGER BABIES

Tiger cubs are born small and helpless, but the mother must leave them alone while she hunts. Tiger cubs hunt on their own when they are two years old.

Siberian Tiger

Tiger Talk	
CHUFFLE:	"Hello," or sometimes, "I'm so happy."
GRRRR:	"This is my territory" or a male calling a female
ROARRR:	"I'm warning you!"

WHERE IN THE WORLD ARE TIGERS?

RANGE: small pockets of Asia

HABITAT: tropical rain forests, snow-covered coniferous and deciduous forests, mangrove swamps, and drier forest areas

Lion

Asiatic Lion

LION STUFF

LENGTH: males, 5.6 to 8.3 feet; females, 4.6 to 5.7 feet
TAIL LENGTH: 27 to 41 inches
SHOULDER HEIGHT: males, 4 feet; females, 3.5 feet
WEIGHT: males, 330 to 550 pounds; females, 265 to 400 pounds
LIFE SPAN: 15 years
NUMBER OF YOUNG AT BIRTH: 1 to 6, usually 3 to 4
SIZE AT BIRTH: 3 pounds
CONSERVATION STATUS: Asian lion, vulnerable

LIVING WITH PRIDE

Lions are the only cats who live in large, social groups. A lion pride is made up of three to 30 lions and consists of lionesses (mothers, sisters, and cousins) and their cubs, along with a few unrelated adult males. Members of the pride have close bonds and are not likely to accept a stranger. The unrelated males stay a few months or a few years, but the older lionesses stay together for life. In dry areas with less food, prides are smaller, with two lionesses in charge. With more food and water, prides can have four to six adult lionesses.

NOT ALL CATS ARE ALIKE

Lions are the only members of the cat family to have males and females that look

Super Bowl Hero
A lion chasing down prey can run the length of a football field in SIX SECONDS.

distinctly different. Only lions have a tuft of dark hairs on the tips of their tails, which helps them communicate with other lions in their pride.

Female Transvaal Lion

ALL FOR YAWN AND YAWN FOR ALL

Lion researchers have noticed that some activities are contagious in prides. One lion will yawn, or groom itself, or roar, setting off a wave of yawning, grooming, or roaring!

WHERE IN THE WORLD ARE LIONS?

RANGE: parts of Africa and India's Gir Forest

HABITAT: grassy plains, savannas, open woodlands, and scrublands

Female and Male Transvaal Lions

Male Transvaal Lion

KING OF THE BEASTS

Male lions eat more than the lionesses but bring in far less food (males hunt less than 10 percent of the time). But the males patrol, mark, and guard the pride's territory. Males also baby-sit with the cubs while the lionesses are out hunting. When new males try to join a pride, they have to fight the males already there. The lion's thick mane protects his neck against raking claws during fights.

JUST LION AROUND

A lion's life is filled with sleeping, napping, and resting. Over the course of 24 hours, lions have short bursts of intense activity, followed by long bouts of lying around that total up to 21 hours! Lions are good climbers and often rest in trees, perhaps to catch a cool breeze or to get away from flies. Researchers have often noticed lions lying around in crazy poses, on their backs with their feet in the air or legs spread wide open.

Juvenile Transvaal Lions

YOU GO, GIRLS!

Lions live in a matriarchal society. The lionesses work together to hunt and rear the cubs. During hunting, smaller females chase the prey toward the larger and heavier lionesses who ambush it.

AN EATING MACHINE

Lions digest their food so quickly they can eat a second helping shortly after gorging themselves on dinner. They hunt antelope and hoofed animals, baby elephants or rhinos, rodents, reptiles, insects, crocodiles, and even buffalo and giraffes. Lions will steal prey from leopards, cheetahs, hyenas, or wild dogs. They will even eat prey that has spoiled.

Male Transvaal Lion

Leopard

LEOPARD STUFF

LENGTH: 3 to 6 feet
TAIL LENGTH: 23 to 44 inches
WEIGHT: males, 80 to 200 pounds; females, 62 to 132 pounds
LIFE SPAN: 12 to 15 years in the wild
NUMBER OF YOUNG AT BIRTH: 1 to 6, usually 2 to 3
SIZE AT BIRTH: 1 pound
CONSERVATION STATUS: all 8 subspecies endangered

North Chinese Leopard

SUPERCAT!

Leopards are strong swimmers, can run in bursts up to 36 miles an hour, leap 20 feet forward in a single bound, jump 10 feet straight up in the air, and climb 50 feet up a tree while holding a dead animal in its mouth, even one larger and heavier than itself.

Persian Leopard Rosettes

SEEING SPOTS

Leopards have spots on their backs called rosettes. White spots on the tips of their tails and backs of their ears help leopards locate and communicate with each other in tall grass. Nearly black leopards live in the thick rain forests of Southeast Asia. They may look solid black, but they have a black-on-black rosette-patterned coat.

Persian Leopard

Indochinese Leopard

Snow Leopard

Clouded Leopard

North Chinese Leopard

A MIDNIGHT SNACK

Since leopards hunt at night, they use their vision and keen hearing. They stalk and pounce, grabbing their prey by the throat. Leopards are carnivores and will eat any meat they can get: monkeys, baboons, rodents, reptiles, amphibians, large birds, fish, antelope, cheetah cubs, and porcupines.

WHEN IS A LEOPARD NOT A LEOPARD?

Although both snow leopards and clouded leopards have leopard in their common names, they are different enough from the true leopards to have their own classifications within the cat family.

STALK, POUNCE, AND CHASE

Have you ever seen a housecat creep slowly after a bird or mouse? That's stalking. A quick leap and a grab with the claws is a pounce, and the chase begins if the prey gets away. Leopard cubs play stalk, pounce, and chase with their brothers, sisters, and even their mother. This is how they learn to hunt for food.

WHERE IN THE WORLD ARE LEOPARDS?

RANGE: Africa and Asia

HABITAT: forests, mountains, grasslands, and deserts

No Thanks, I'm Not Thirsty
The Persian leopard can live without ever drinking water. It gets the moisture it needs from food.

LENGTH: 18 to 30 inches
WEIGHT: males, 121 pounds; females, 79 pounds
LIFE SPAN: 12 to 15 years
NUMBER OF YOUNG AT BIRTH: 1 to 4
SIZE AT BIRTH: 1.5 to 2 pounds
CONSERVATION STATUS: endangered

Heavyweight Contender
Jaguars are the largest cats in the Western Hemisphere and the third largest overall. Only lions and tigers are bigger.

WHERE IN THE WORLD ARE JAGUARS?

RANGE: North, Central, and South America

HABITAT: rain forests, swampy areas, grasslands, woodlands, dry forests, and even deserts

JAGUAR OR LEOPARD?

Jaguars and leopards look a lot alike, but there are ways to tell them apart. Jaguars are stockier and heavier, with shorter, thicker tails. They have dark spots on their backs, called rosettes, with an irregular border and often a spot in the center. Leopards also have dark rosettes on a tawny coat, but if you look closely at each rosette, you'll see that there is no spot inside, and the rosette edge is broken.

A ROARING GOOD TIME

There are four big cats in the biological group *Panthera*: jaguars, lions, tigers, and leopards. These are the only big cats that can roar. They roar to scare off other animals and defend their territory.

THE EYES HAVE IT

Like other cats, jaguars have eyes that see best at night. Eyeshine is caused by a mirror-like structure in the back of their eye that reflects light into the retina and doubles their night vision.

A LEISURELY DINNER

Jaguars stalk and ambush their ground-dwelling prey at night, instead of chasing it as cheetahs and lions do. Their large jaw muscles allow them to eat hard-shelled reptiles like turtles and tortoises. The jaguar diet includes peccaries, deer, tapirs, and cattle.

What's a Black Panther?
There is no animal named "black panther." "Panther" is a term that comes from the Panthera animal group name.

CAMO-FUR

Most jaguars have tawny-colored fur with black rosettes that helps the animal hide in the tall grass. Jaguars living in darker rain forest areas are black on black.

Gone Fishin'
Jaguars are at home in the water, and stay near rivers and lakes. A jaguar waves its tail over the water to attract hungry fish for dinner.

A RUNNING MACHINE

Cheetahs have a flexible spine, which allows their front legs to stretch far forward on each stride. While running, they cover 20 to 22 feet with each stride. Cheetahs are off the ground more than half of their running time. They can run up to 70 miles per hour.

DO YOU HEAR WHAT I HEAR?

Cheetahs are quite vocal, making a unique, bird-like sound called a chirrup when they're excited. Mothers use the same sound to call their cubs. They also purr, growl, snarl, hiss, cough, moan, and bleat. Cheetahs cannot roar like lions or tigers. Researchers have learned that, during mating season, cheetahs make a unique sound called a stutter bark.

GRAB A QUICK BITE

Cheetahs must eat quickly because they aren't strong enough to hide or guard their catch. They kill more often and eat only the meat (not skin or bones) of antelope, birds, rabbits, porcupines, and ostriches.

A LITTLE RUN BEFORE DINNER

While sprinting, cheetahs can turn in midair to follow their prey. Once the cheetah catches its prey, it latches onto its neck. By now the cheetah is panting intensely and its body temperature may be as high as 105°F. It takes 20 minutes for the cheetah's breathing and temperature to return to normal which is the same amount of time it will take for the prey to suffocate. Cheetahs have smaller teeth and larger nasal passages than other big cats, which allows them to take in more air during the recovery period after a sprint.

WHERE IN THE WORLD ARE CHEETAHS?

RANGE: Parts of Africa; a small group lives in Iran

HABITAT: grasslands and open plains

Mother and Cub

NOT MUCH SOCIAL LIFE

Cheetahs are solitary and peaceable except at breeding time, when males fight over females and have been known to kill each other. Cubs live with their mothers for about 18 months. Litter mates will stay together for six to eight more months. Then the females head off to live on their own, while the males stay together in small groups until they are mature.

Snow Leopard

A TALE OF A TAIL

The snow leopard's incredibly long and beautiful tail helps with balance and is sometimes as long as the cat's body. This long, thick, and luxurious tail acts as a built-in comforter when the leopard wraps it around its body for added warmth.

LIFE AT THE TOP OF THE WORLD

Snow leopards are rarely seen in the wild. They are almost impossible to locate and study because of their secretive behavior, their ability to blend in with their surroundings, and their remote habitat among the highest mountains in the world. The extreme conditions and steep terrain of their habitat, often beyond the limits of human endurance, make it difficult to trap and radio tag snow leopards for research purposes.

WHAT'S FOR DINNER?

Snow leopards are capable of killing prey up to two to three times their own weight. Recent radio-tracking data shows they bring down prey every 10 to 15 days. Blue sheep and ibex are their main prey, along with marmots, game birds, small rodents, and livestock.

Jumping Jacks

Snow leopards can jump and pounce on prey up to 45 feet away! They need to be great leapers and jumpers to travel between the cliffs and ravines of their home.

A HOME IN THE SKY

Snow leopards have been seen at altitudes as high as 18,000 feet in summer. That's only a few thousand feet short of the top of Mount Everest!

Snow Leopard Cub

ADVERTISING FOR A BRIDE

It isn't easy for snow leopards to find each another, so the cats leave distinct signals along their routes. The cats leave their scent and rake their claws on boulders and tree trunks. They deposit urine and feces in soil depressions. They run their cheeks on rocks, trees, and the ground. All of these "advertisements" mark their range. When breeding season arrives, January through late March, the cats call to one another.

OH BABY, BABY

When it's time for the cubs to be born, the mother snow leopard looks for a safe place to have and rear them. Usually two or three cubs are born. The cubs' eyes open when they are about seven days old and by three months they learn how to hunt for food.

GHOST CAT

Because of their shy behavior and uncanny, almost mystical ability to disappear among the rocks, snow leopards are thought by some people to be shape-changing mountain spirits.

FEARFULLY AND WONDERFULLY MADE

Snow leopards are specially built to live at high altitudes. They have a relatively small head, but their short, broad nose has a large nasal cavity that passes cold air through and warms it. Huge paws with fur on the bottoms protect and cushion their feet and provide traction on snow. Short, well-developed front legs and chest muscles help with balance when climbing. Smoky gray and blurred black markings provide camouflage in the mountains.

WHERE IN THE WORLD ARE SNOW LEOPARDS?

RANGE: the mountains of Central Asia

HABITAT: cliffs, rocky slopes, and coniferous forest scrublands

Polar Bear

POLAR BEAR STUFF

LENGTH: 6.6 to 10 feet
SHOULDER HEIGHT: to 5.3 feet
WEIGHT: males, 660 to 1,760 pounds; females, 330 to 660 pounds
LIFE SPAN: 25 to 30 years
NUMBER OF YOUNG AT BIRTH: 1 to 4, usually 2
SIZE AT BIRTH: 1.3 pounds
CONSERVATION STATUS: vulnerable

FROZEN FOOD

Polar bears are mainly meat eaters, and their favorite food is seal. They will also eat walrus, caribou, beached whales, grass, and seaweed. Polar bears are patient hunters, staying motionless for hours above a seal's breathing hole in the ice, just waiting for dinner to pop up.

BUTTON UP YOUR OVERCOAT

Polar bears look white, but their hair is really clear, hollow tubes filled with air. These long hairs stick together when wet and form a waterproof barrier that keeps the thick, furry undercoat dry.

WHERE IN THE WORLD ARE POLAR BEARS?

RANGE: along the coasts and inland streams and lakes of Alaska, Canada, Greenland, Norway, and Russia

HABITAT: Arctic tundras, and wooded habitats

WE'RE HAVING A HEAT WAVE

Polar bears are built to stay so warm in their cold habitat that sometimes they overheat and have to cool off in the icy water.

Mother and Cub

Mother and Cub

NAP TIME

Polar bears do not hibernate when the temperature drops, but their bodily functions slow down. Many scientists call this "winter sleep," because the bears can easily be awakened. A mother polar bear can give birth and nurse her young during winter sleep.

Nose on Legs

The polar bear can smell a seal on the ice 20 miles away, sniff out a seal's den covered with snow, and find a seal's air hole in the ice up to a mile away.

BABY, IT'S COLD OUTSIDE!

Polar bears have blubber two to four inches thick that insulates the bears from the freezing air and cold water. Blubber is also a nutritional reserve and it helps the bears float in the water, sort of like an inner tube.

DEN MOTHER

A mother polar bear digs a den in the snow about the size of a telephone booth. Usually two cubs are born in December or January and are about the size of a rat, hairless, and blind. By April they are more than 20 pounds. When the cubs are two years old, they are ready to be on their own.

Giant Panda

WHAT HAPPENED TO DINNER?

When bamboo plants reach maturity, they flower and produce seeds, and then the plant dies. All of the plants of a species will bloom and die at the same time. When those plants die, pandas must move to another area to find another species of bamboo. As their habitat shrinks, pandas are often unable to move to another area.

A Bachelor Life for Me
Pandas live alone except at mating time.

BLACK AND WHITE AND LOVED ALL OVER

The giant panda is a national treasure in China and is protected by law. This unique bear has long been revered by the Chinese and can be found in Chinese art dating back thousands of years.

Giant Panda Bears
The genetic code (DNA) in pandas' cells confirm that pandas are bears.

Mother and One-and-a-half-year-old Panda

GYMNASTICS

Giant pandas are curious and playful, especially when they're young. They have unusually thick and heavy bones for their size, but they are very flexible and love to do somersaults.

Mother and Four-and-a-half-month-old Cub

What's for Dinner?
Giant pandas live mostly on bamboo.

EATING AGAIN?

Pandas live in cold and rainy bamboo forests high in the mountains of western China. They spend at least 12 hours a day eating. Because bamboo is so low in nutrients, pandas must eat as much as 84 pounds of it each day.

HOW TO EAT A BAMBOO STALK

A panda grasps the bamboo stalk with five fingers and a special wristbone. Teeth peel off the tough outer layers of the bamboo stalk to get to the soft inner tissue. Now the panda bites down on the thick stalk with its strong jaw and chews. For an appetizer, the panda strips leaves off the bamboo stalks, wads them up, and swallows them whole. For a change, the giant panda occasionally eats grasses, bulbs, fruits, some insects, and even rodents.

WHERE IN THE WORLD ARE GIANT PANDAS?

Where, Oh Where, Is a Panda Bear?
Today, only around 1,600 giant pandas survive in the wild.

RANGE: southwestern China, in six small forests

HABITAT: damp, misty forests of bamboo and conifers, in altitudes above 4,000 feet

WHAT DID YOU SAY?

Pandas make a bleating sound similar to that of a lamb or goat kid. They also honk, huff, bark, or growl. Young cubs croak and squeal.

TINY GIANT

When born, giant pandas are about the size of a stick of butter. They have no fur and are completely helpless. The panda mother cares for her tiny cub. She cradles it in one paw and holds it close to her chest. For several days after birth, the mother does not leave the den, not even to eat or drink.

Mother and Four-month-old Cub

Brown Bear

BROWN BEAR STUFF

LENGTH: 6 to 9.8 feet
SHOULDER HEIGHT: 3 to 4 feet
WEIGHT: males, 330 to 1,500 pounds; females, 215 to 660 pounds
LIFE SPAN: 25 years in the wild, to 40 years in zoos
CONSERVATION STATUS: overall, numbers are declining; certain local populations, endangered or threatened

Alaskan Brown Bear

WHERE IN THE WORLD ARE BROWN BEARS?

RANGE: North America, Asia, Europe, Africa, and the Middle East

HABITAT: Temperate and coniferous forest, open fields, mountain highlands, and tundra

Humpbacks

Large shoulder muscles give brown bears a prominent hump. Brown bears' snouts slope upward sharply to the forehead, creating a dish-shaped face.

WHAT COLOR IS A BROWN BEAR?

Brown bears come in many colors. Some brown bears really do have brown coats, but others run the color spectrum from cream-colored to almost black. The medium-sized brown bears of the Rocky Mountains, also known as grizzly bears, were named for the silver-tipped sheen of their fur.

Grizzly Bear

Alaskan Brown Bear

WHERE HAVE ALL THE BROWN BEARS GONE?

Fewer than 200 years ago, brown bears inhabited such seemingly unbearlike places as Mexico and northern Africa. Today, although their range is still vast, brown bears are rare in terms of absolute numbers.

Alaskan Brown Bear

GIANTS WALK THE EARTH

Kodiak bears (bears from Kodiak Island on the coastal Alaskan mainland) and Alaskan brown bears can weigh in excess of 1,200 pounds. These kinds of bears are some of the largest in the world. Only polar bears can grow larger.

Alaskan Brown Bear

Alaskan Brown Bear

GONE FISHIN'

Brown bears fatten up on salmon they catch with their quick claws and strong jaws. These same powerful weapons allow brown bears to successfully hunt animals as large as moose.

Alaskan Brown Bear

What's for Dinner? Brown bears will eat almost anything. But the bulk of their diet is berries, nuts, and roots.

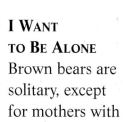

I WANT TO BE ALONE

Brown bears are solitary, except for mothers with cubs, but do not appear to be territorial. Large numbers of bears form at feeding areas and fights break out. Large adult males tend to be the leaders.

Malayan Sun Bear

WEIGHT: 60 to 145 pounds
LIFE SPAN: unknown
NUMBER OF YOUNG: 1 to 3
SIZE AT BIRTH: 7 to 12 ounces
CONSERVATION STATUS: at critical risk

Malayan Sun Bear

DON'T MESS WITH A SUN BEAR

The sun bears' claws and canine teeth are strong weapons in a fight. If an enemy hangs on during the fight, the sun bear can turn inside its loose skin and bite its attacker. Even though they live in a hot, humid climate, their fur is unusually thick and dense and will protect the sun bear.

Everybody Has a Nickname
"Dog bear," "Malay bear," and "honey bear" are common nicknames for the sun bear.

WHERE IN THE WORLD ARE SUN BEARS?

RANGE: Thailand, Cambodia, Vietnam, Laos, Burma, the Malay Peninsula, Sumatra, and Borneo

HABITAT: dense tropical and subtropical forests

Malayan Sun Bear

Malayan Sun Bear

CUB SCOUTING

Sun bears build a nest in leafy vegetation on the ground or hollow logs. Cubs are born hairless, unable to hear or smell, and dependent upon their mother for food, warmth, and protection. By two months of age, the youngsters are able to run and play. They will stay with their mother for the next two years. Mother sun bears sometimes walk upright and carry their babies in their arms.

No Time to Rest
Since they live in a tropical environment, sun bears do not hibernate.

Bornean Sun Bear

A SWEET LUNCH

The omnivorous sun bear uses its front paws and long claws to rip open trees in search of insects, honey, or sap which it scoops up with a very long tongue. Other food choices include fruit, honey, small birds, lizards, rodents, and coconuts, which it opens with its jaws and teeth.

Malayan Sun Bear

Bornean Sun Bear

Elephants

AFRICAN ELEPHANT STUFF

SHOULDER HEIGHT: males, 10.5 to 13 feet; females, 8.2 feet

WEIGHT: males, to 15,000 pounds (7.5 tons); females, to 8,000 pounds (4 tons)

LIFE SPAN: may live more than 50 years

NUMBER OF YOUNG AT BIRTH: 1

WEIGHT AT BIRTH: 117 to 330 pounds, average 232 pounds

HEIGHT AT BIRTH: 26 to 42 inches

CONSERVATION STATUS: African forest elephant endangered

African Elephant

WHERE IN THE WORLD ARE AFRICAN ELEPHANTS?

RANGE: Kenya, Zimbabwe, Tanzania, Zambia, Uganda, Democratic Republic of the Congo, Namibia, and national parks in South Africa

HABITAT: grassland savannas and open woodlands

Drink 480 Glasses of Water a Day
Elephants drink about 30 gallons of water EVERY day.

African or Asian?

There are 2 different kinds of elephants: African and Asian. Can you tell them apart?

African Elephants	Asian Elephants
• have large ears shaped like the continent of Africa	• have smaller ears
• both males and females have visible tusks	• only the males have visible tusks
• their skin is very wrinkly	• their skin is not as wrinkled
• their backs are swayed	• their backs are dome-shaped.
• the end of their trunk works as if they have 2 fingers there to help them pick things up.	• they only have 1 "finger" at the end of their trunks

SHOULDER HEIGHT: 8.2 to 9.8 feet
WEIGHT: males, 11,000 pounds (5.5 tons); females, 6,000 pounds (3 tons)
LIFE SPAN: may live more than 50 years
NUMBER OF YOUNG AT BIRTH: 1
WEIGHT AT BIRTH: 110 to 250 pounds
CONSERVATION STATUS: endangered

Bigger Than Dumbo

The largest elephant on record was an adult male African elephant. It weighed about 24,000 pounds (12 tons) and was 13 feet tall at the shoulder!

OH MAMA!

Both African and Asian elephants live in herds made up of related females, called cows, and their offspring. The leader of the herd is the matriarch, usually the oldest and most experienced female. The matriarch decides when and where the herd will eat, rest, and travel.

Asian Elephant

PLACES TO GO, THINGS TO DO

Adult males, called bulls, don't live in a herd. Once male elephants become teenagers, they leave the herd. Only after they become adults will they visit other herds, and that is only for short periods of time to mate. Bulls do not take part in caring for the young.

WHERE IN THE WORLD ARE ASIAN ELEPHANTS?

RANGE: India, Nepal, and Southeast Asia

HABITAT: scrub forests and edges of rain forests

African Elephant Herd

Asian Elephant

TOOTH AND TUSK

Tusks are an elephant's incisor teeth. They are used for defense, digging for water, and lifting things. Elephants also have four molars. One molar can weigh about five pounds and is the size of a brick. Each elephant can go through six sets of molars in a lifetime.

Asian Elephant

Million-Dollar Teeth
Elephants have been relentlessly hunted for their tusks, even though the tusks are made of dentine–the same as our teeth.

Can You Hear Me Now?
The calls elephants make can be heard by another elephant up to five miles away.

BABY ELEPHANT WALK

A baby elephant, called a calf, may be three feet tall when born. Calves are clumsy at using their trunks. But as they grow, they get the hang of the trunk.

THICK SKIN, SOFT HEART

Pachyderm means "thick skin" and refers to both elephants and hippopotamuses. An elephant's skin can be up to one inch thick, but it is so sensitive that the elephant can feel a fly. To protect their skin, elephants spray themselves with water or roll in the mud or dust for protection.

African Elephant Drinking

18-day-old African Elephant

IF I ONLY HAD A STRAW

Elephants use their trunks to drink, but the water doesn't go all the way up the trunk like a straw. Instead, the elephant sucks water part way up the trunk, curls it toward its mouth, tilts its head up, and lets the water pour in.

Asian Elephant

African Elephant

Are You Hungry?
Stomach growls are welcome in polite elephant society. Their stomachs make loud rumbling and growling noises that signal "everything is a-okay."

Eat Plenty of Fiber
Elephants eat 220 to 440 pounds of vegetation every day. They like grass, fruit, leaves, and even tree bark.

COOL EARS
Elephants' ears are air conditioners. Flapping their ears on a hot day cools the blood flowing through their ears. This in turn, cools their bodies.

THE NOSE KNOWS
There are more than 40,000 muscles in the trunk. (That's more muscles than in the human body!) An elephant's trunk is so strong it can push down trees, but so agile it can pick up a single piece of straw.

Asian Elephants

Asian Elephant

WHERE DOES AN OLD ELEPHANT GO?
When elephants get old, their teeth become sensitive, so they eat softer food. Marshes are the perfect place for soft plant food, so old elephants are often found there. Many times they stay until they die. This led some people to think that elephants went to special burial grounds to die.

Hippopotamus

Mother and Calf

WHERE IN THE WORLD ARE HIPPOPOTAMUSES?

RANGE: western, central, eastern, and southern Africa

HABITAT: lakes, swamps, and slow-flowing rivers

WHAT'S IN A NAME?

Hippopotamus comes from a Greek word meaning "water or river horse." But hippos are not related to horses at all. In fact, they are thought to be most closely related to Cetaceans (whales).

Mother and Calf

OH BABY, BABY

Hippo calves are born underwater. They must quickly get to the top to catch their first breath, close their nostrils as their parents do, and then submerge to nurse.

What's That I "Herd?"
Common river hippos live in herds of about 10 to 30 animals, but they have been observed in groups as large as 100.

COME ON IN, THE WATER'S FINE!

Hippos cannot swim. Their bodies are too dense to float. They push off from the riverbed or simply walk along the river bottom in a slow-motion gallop, lightly touching the bottom with their toes like aquatic ballet dancers.

Mother and Calf

NIGHTTIME IS DINNERTIME

Hippos spend most of the hot days wallowing in shallow water. After sunset, hippos come out of the water to graze on the long grass. A single hippo can eat up to 100 pounds of grass in a single night. Before sunrise, the hippos return to the cool water.

Rhinoceros

Southern Black Rhinoceros

DRESSED FOR BATTLE

Asian rhinos look like they are covered in armor, but they are actually covered with a layer of skin that has many folds. Also called "the greater one-horned rhino," they are native to swampy areas of Northeast India and Nepal.

We're Coming Through!

A group of rhinos is called a crash, appropriate for a large animal that can crash through just about anything in its way.

WHAT'S IN A NAME?

Rhinoceroses get their name from their most famous feature: their horns. The word rhinoceros comes from the Greek *rhino* (nose) and *ceros* (horn). Like our fingernails and hair, rhino horn is made of keratin. The five types of rhinos are the Sumatran, Javan, black, white, and Indian. Javan and Indian rhinos have only one horn, while Sumatran, black, and white rhinos have two.

Indian Rhinoceros Mother and Calf

East African Black Rhinoceros

White Rhinoceros

WHAT'S A RHINO?

All rhinos have large heads, broad chests, thick legs, poor eyesight, excellent hearing, and a fondness for rolling in the mud. They are very nearsighted and often charge when they are startled. Rhinos eat grass or leaves.

Get Outta My Way!
A black rhino can thunder along at 40 miles per hour.

BLACK AND WHITE AND GRAY ALL OVER

Black rhinos and white rhinos are actually the same color: brownish gray. The white rhino has a wide mouth perfect for grazing on grasses. The black rhino has a narrower lip, good for pulling leaves and shrubs into its mouth. Other names used for these rhinos are "broad-lipped," for the white rhino, and "hook-lipped," for the black rhino.

IN TOUCH WITH YOUR SENSITIVE HIDE

The rhino's skin is quite sensitive, especially to sunburn and biting insects. That's why they like to wallow in mud.

Southern White Rhinoceroses

WHERE IN THE WORLD ARE RHINOCEROSES?

RANGE: white rhinos and black rhinos, small pockets of eastern and southern Africa; Indian rhinos, northern India and southern Nepal; Sumatran and Javan rhinos, small areas of Vietnam, Malaysia, and Indonesia

HABITAT: open grasslands and floodplains for black rhinos and white rhinos; swamps and forests for Indian, Javan, and Sumatran rhinos

HE'S GOT SUCH A BIG HEAD

White rhinos have a hump of muscle on their necks and shoulders to hold up a head that can weigh 2,000 pounds (1 ton).

Mammals 163

SHOULDER HEIGHT: 5.9 to 7.5 feet
WEIGHT: 660 to 1,520 pounds
LIFE SPAN: up to 50 years
NUMBER OF YOUNG AT BIRTH: 1
WEIGHT AT BIRTH: 80 pounds
CONSERVATION STATUS: wild Bactrian camel at critical risk

Dromedary Camel

Bactrian Camel

Bactrian Camel

AT HOME IN THE SAND

Double rows of extra-long eyelashes protect the eyes from blowing sand. The eye has a thin membrane, like a clear inner eyelid, that shields the eye. Camels close their nostrils to keep sand out of their noses; and their large, broad feet keep the camel from sinking in the sand.

Are You Thirsty?
Camels can go a week or more without water. Then they drink up to 32 gallons of water at one time.

WHERE IN THE WORLD ARE CAMELS?

RANGE: Bactrian camels in China and Mongolia; dromedary camels currently in domestic situations only, but once native to North Africa and the Middle East

HABITAT: deserts, prairies, and steppes

164 **Mammals**

Dromedary Camel

Bactrian Camel

One Hump or Two?

The dromedary camel has one hump. The Bactrian camel has two. The humps are stored fat. Camels can go several months without food. As the camel uses the fat in the hump, it begins to droop.

WHAT DID YOU SAY?

Camels make many sounds, including moaning and groaning sounds, high-pitched bleats, and loud bellows and roars. They also make a rumbling growl that was one of the noises used to create Chewbacca's voice in the *Star Wars* movies.

Ships of the Desert

Camels can carry 200 pounds and walk 20 miles a day in the desert.

Bactrian Camels

Bactrian Camels

SPITTING IS SO RUDE!

Camels don't really spit. It's more like throwing up. Camels regurgitate the contents of their stomachs, along with saliva, and project it out. This is meant to surprise, distract, or bother whatever threatens the camel.

MOVIN' AND GROOVIN'

Camels have a natural pacing gait, moving both legs from the same side of the body at the same time.

Giraffe

GIRAFFE STUFF

HEIGHT: males, to 18 feet; females, to 14 feet
WEIGHT: males, to 3,000 pounds; females, to 1,500 pounds
LIFE SPAN: 15 to 20 years
NUMBER OF YOUNG AT BIRTH: 1
SIZE AT BIRTH: 6 feet tall, 100 to 150 pounds
CONSERVATION STATUS: lower risk

Masai Giraffe

Masai Giraffe

DROPPING IN

When a giraffe calf is born, it drops to the ground head first, about a six-foot drop. The fall and the landing don't hurt the calf, but they do cause it to take a big breath. The calf can stand up and walk after about an hour. Sometimes the mother will leave the calf alone for most of the day. The youngster sits quietly by itself until she returns.

Young Masai Giraffe

A LOT OF HEART

A giraffe's heart is two feet long and weighs about 25 pounds. Giraffe lungs can hold 12 gallons of air.

LONG TONGUE

A giraffe's tongue is 18 to 20 inches long and blue-black. The color may keep the tongue from getting sunburned.

What Did You Say?
Giraffes can moo, hiss, roar, and whistle.

STAND UP STRAIGHT

There are seven vertebrae in a giraffe's neck, the same as humans. Each giraffe vertebra is over 10 inches long. A giraffe's six-foot neck weighs about 600 pounds!

WHERE IN THE WORLD ARE GIRAFFES?

RANGE: pockets of Africa, south of the Sahara Desert

HABITAT: savannas

Uganda/Baringo Giraffe

Masai Giraffe

HELLO, UP THERE!

Giraffes are the tallest land animals. Their legs are six feet long. The back legs look shorter than the front legs, but they are about the same length.

LUMPY HEAD

Both male and female giraffes have two distinct, hair-covered horns called *ossicones*. Male giraffes use their horns to playfully fight with one another. As male giraffes age, calcium deposits form on their skulls and other horn-like bumps develop.

Uganda/Baringo Giraffe

Want to Race?
The record running speed of a giraffe is 34.7 miles per hour.

EATING THE TREES

Giraffes eat up to 75 pounds of leaves each day. They spend most of their day eating because they get just a few leaves in each bite.

Masai Giraffe

CHEW IT AGAIN AND AGAIN!

The giraffe is a ruminant and has a stomach with four compartments that digests the leaves it eats. When giraffes aren't eating, they are chewing their cud. After they swallow the leaves the first time, a ball of leaves will travel all the way back up the throat into the mouth for more grinding.

PACE YOURSELF

When giraffes walk or run, both the front and back legs on one side move forward together, then the other two legs on the other side move forward. This is called pacing.

TAIL

The giraffe has the longest tail of any land mammal. Tails can be eight feet long, including the tuft.

WEIGHT: 550 to 900 pounds
LIFE SPAN: 25 years
NUMBER OF YOUNG AT BIRTH: 1
SIZE AT BIRTH: 55 to 88 pounds
CONSERVATION STATUS: Grevy's zebra and mountain zebra endangered

SEEING STRIPES

Each zebra has a unique stripe pattern. When zebras are huddled together, their stripes make it hard for a lion to pick out one zebra to chase. Different zebra species have different types of stripes, from narrow to wide. When stripes are painted on a wall, a zebra will stand next to them.

Hartmann's Mountain Zebra

LAWN MOWERS

Zebras eat grass and leaves and stems of bushes. Their strong front teeth clip off the tips and their back teeth crush and grind the food. Chewing wears the zebra's teeth down, but their teeth continue to grow.

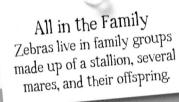

All in the Family
Zebras live in family groups made up of a stallion, several mares, and their offspring.

WHERE IN THE WORLD ARE ZEBRAS?

RANGE: eastern and southern Africa

HABITAT: grasslands and savannas

GET YOUR KICKS

Zebras have excellent hearing and eyesight and can run at speeds of up to 35 miles per hour. Their powerful kicks can injure a lion. The stallion stays at the back of the group to defend against predators, while the mares and foals run from danger.

RUN, ZEBRA, RUN!

Zebra foals are dark brown and white at birth. They can run one hour after birth. The mare must remain with the group and cannot leave the foal. It must be up and running quickly in order to stay with its mother.

Damara Zebra

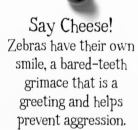

Hartmann's Mountain Zebra

SCRATCH MY BACK AND I'LL SCRATCH YOURS

When zebras stand head to back, apparently biting each other, they are actually nibbling on each other to pull out loose hair and give each other a good scratch.

SPLISH, SPLASH, OH, WHAT A BATH

Zebras take dust or mud baths. They shake the dirt off to get rid of loose hair and flaky skin. What's left protects them from sun, wind, and insects.

Say Cheese!
Zebras have their own smile, a bared-teeth grimace that is a greeting and helps prevent aggression.

Damara Zebra

Damara Zebra

BETTER CLOSE YOUR MOUTH!

Zebras communicate with loud braying, barking, and soft snorting or *whuffling*. The position of their ears, how wide open their eyes are, and whether their mouths are open or their teeth bared all mean something to other zebras.

Wolf

WOLF STUFF

LENGTH: 4.5 to 6.5 feet
WEIGHT: 60 to 100 pounds
LIFE SPAN: 13 to 15 years
NUMBER OF YOUNG AT BIRTH: 4 to 6
SIZE AT BIRTH: 1 pound
CONSERVATION STATUS: timber wolf endangered

Mexican Gray Wolf

ON THE ROAD AGAIN

Wolves travel long distances at a regular trot of about five miles per hour. They move faster when they are on a hunt. Wolves sometimes travel hundreds of miles from their home territory in search of food.

EIGHT-PACK

Wolves live in family groups called packs. A pack consists of an adult male and female and their pups. The average size of a pack is eight or nine, but packs can occasionally get as large as 20 to 30.

ALPHA ONE? THIS IS ALPHA TWO.

Each wolf pack has a head male and female, called alphas. Only the alpha female has pups. The alphas are usually the oldest and strongest members of the pack and organize the pack to hunt as a group.

British Columbian Wolves

WHERE DO WOLVES LIVE?

Wolves' territories can be as small as 20 square miles or as large as 1,000 square miles. Wolves avoid people if they can. Loss of habitat is the main reason for the decline of wolves in some parts of the world.

Canadian Gray Wolf

I'LL TELL YOU HOW I FEEL

Wolves bare their teeth and growl if they are angry. The leader holds its tail high. They lower their bodies and tails to show submission. If they flatten their ears, they are afraid. And wolves howl. Some researchers believe wolves howl for fun or to call a hunt.

Play Toss-the-Bone
Wolves love to play. They begin with a bow to each other. Then they toss toys to each other like bones or sticks.

Chinese or Golden Wolf

IT TAKES A VILLAGE

All of the members in a wolf pack take care of the babies. They bring them food, play with them, and act as baby-sitters.

Canadian Gray Wolf

LET THEM EAT STEAK

Wolves are meat eaters. They prefer large prey such as goats, sheep, or deer, which they kill with their strong jaws. Wolves work as a team to attack these large animals. When they find food, they gorge themselves, because it might be days before they eat again.

WHERE IN THE WORLD ARE WOLVES?

RANGE: North America, northern Europe, and Asia

HABITAT: wilderness areas

British Columbian Gray Wolf

Kangaroo & Wallaby

Eastern Red Kangaroo

THE BIG GUYS

The red kangaroo, found most often on the open plains of inland Australia, can live on very little water. With dark red fur and a white face and belly, males are often referred to as red flyers. Red kangaroos can be over six feet tall and weigh up to 200 pounds. When spooked, they can leap across the outback in 10-foot-high, 39-foot-long bounds.

MYSTERIOUS MAMMAL MOVEMENT

When the kangaroo hops, both feet push off the ground at the same time. The larger kangaroos can cover over 15 feet per hop when cruising at top speed and have been clocked at more than 30 miles per hour in short bursts.

Western Gray Kangaroo

WHERE IN THE WORLD ARE KANGAROOS & WALLABIES?

RANGE: Australia and New Guinea

HABITAT: every habitat in Australia and wet forests in New Guinea

Eastern Gray Kangaroo Feet

BIG FEET

The kangaroo's family name, *Macropodidae*, means "big feet," a great description for kangaroos and their relatives. Kangaroos, wallabies, wallaroos, quokkas, pademelons, potoroos, rat-kangaroos, honey possums, and tree kangaroos are all macropods.

Mob Scene
A group of kangaroos is called a mob, a troop, or a herd. They are very social animals.

Troop of Gray Kangaroos

Parma Wallaby

Play It Forward
Kangaroos cannot walk backwards.

HAVE LEGS, WILL HOP

Kangaroos, wallaroos, and wallabies have back legs and feet that are much larger and more powerful than their front legs. Their tails are long, muscular, and thick at the base; the tail helps the animal balance and turn during hopping and provides support when the animal rests.

WHAT'S THE DIFFERENCE?

What's the difference between kangaroos, wallaroos, and wallabies? The main difference between a kangaroo and all the others is size. The largest species are referred to as kangaroos.

Gray Kangaroos

Big Mama
A female kangaroo is called a doe, flyer, jill, or roo.

Big Daddy
A male kangaroo is called a buck, boomer, jack, or old man

New South Wales Wallaroo

HOME, SWEET POUCH

A newborn kangaroo is tiny and underdeveloped. The doe carries the newborn in a special pouch, called a marsupium, on her body. The joey stays in the pouch for several months, just drinking mother's milk. Joeys often peek their heads out of the pouch to have a look around weeks before they head out on their own.

Parma Wallabies

POTTY TRAINING

Do the joeys pee and poop in the pouch? Yes they do! When they are very small they don't produce much. When they get bigger, some is absorbed through the pouch lining. When the pouch gets too smelly, the mother cleans out the pouch.

SAY AGAIN?

A kangaroo's famous jabbing and boxing is sign language. The jab is just one part of a whole vocabulary of glances, hisses, avoidance hops, kicks, punches, gentle touches, and grooming. When a kangaroo senses danger, it alerts its fellows by thumping its feet loudly on the ground. They also communicate with each other by grunting, coughing, or hissing. A doe may make a clicking or clucking sound to call her young.

My, How You've Grown!
Male kangaroos (bucks) keep growing bigger and stronger their whole life.

Southern Yellow-footed Wallaby

New South Wales Wallaroos

EATING AGAIN—AND AGAIN

Kangaroos eat a wide range of plants. All macropods have a chambered stomach. They bring the vegetation they've recently swallowed back up from one chamber, chew it as cud, and then swallow it again for final digestion. Larger kangaroos tend to feed in mobs, though the group size depends on the amount and quality of food that is available.

Mammals 175

Koala

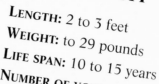

JUST HANGIN' AROUND

Koalas are slow-moving animals that sleep a lot and live in eucalyptus trees. They chew leaves and nap all day.

IS IT A KOALA BEAR?

Koalas have round, fuzzy ears and look like a teddy bear. But koalas are not bears. They are members of a group of pouched animals called marsupials. Koala fur feels like the wool on a sheep.

WHERE IN THE WORLD ARE KOALAS?

RANGE: southeastern and eastern Australia

HABITAT: scrubland eucalyptus forests

Mother and Joey

BABY IN THE POCKET
A newborn koala is called a joey. It is the size of a jellybean, has no fur, and cannot see or hear. Soon after the joey is born, it crawls into its mother's pouch. It will stay there for the next six months. When the joey outgrows the pouch, it will ride on its mother's back. After about a year, it can live alone in the trees.

NOSING AROUND
When a joey learns to eat eucalyptus leaves, it goes after them with its mouth. Its nose gets in the way and pushes the leaves out of reach. Eventually it figures out how to grab leaves with its front paws and put them in its mouth.

Dirt for Dessert
Koalas eat a little dirt now and then to help them digest their eucalyptus leaf meal.

BORN TO CLIMB
A koala has claws on its hands and feet. It has two thumbs on each hand and strong arm and shoulder muscles. Koalas can leap from treetop to treetop.

EUCALYPTUS AGAIN?
Koalas only eat eucalyptus leaves. There are more than 600 different kinds of eucalyptus trees, but koalas prefer the leaves of about three dozen varieties.

Tasmanian Devil

TASMANIAN DEVIL STUFF

LENGTH: 23 to 26 inches; tail about 10 inches
WEIGHT: 13 to 18 pounds
LIFE SPAN: 7 to 8 years
NUMBER AT BIRTH: to 50, but only four can survive in the pouch
SIZE AT BIRTH: about the size of a grain of rice
CONSERVATION STATUS: under Australian government's protection

Clean Up This Mess
Devils will eat anything lying around, no matter how old or rotten.

Male Tasmanian Devil

DEVIL PROTECTION
European settlers to Tasmania in the late 1700s considered Tasmanian devils to be pests because they hunted sheep and ate animals snared in traps. By the 1830s, bounties were placed on the animals until they neared extinction. In 1941 a law was passed protecting devils, and the population has gradually increased.

NOT IN MY FIELDS
Once a year the devil population increases so dramatically that farmers consider them pests. This occurs each summer as the young leave their mothers, but only 40 percent of these young will survive beyond the first few months.

MY BARK IS WORSE THAN MY BITE
Devils have elaborate rituals that often lessen the chances for a fight. Sneezing and nose-to-nose confrontation, during which the devils' ears flush red, are two ways of bluffing. Usually one or both animals will back down.

RACE FOR LIFE
Sometime in April, Mom devil gives birth to about 50 tiny babies, called joeys, each of which is the size of a grain of rice. The joeys must crawl about three inches to Mom's pouch. Only four will have a chance for Mother's milk. The others will die.

WHAT'S FOR DINNER?

Tasmanian devils travel as far as 10 miles each night looking for food. They are carrion eaters, but they also hunt live prey, such as small mammals and birds. Devils hunt at night; by day, they find rest in caves, bushes, old wombat burrows, or hollow logs.

FOOD FIGHT

The devils' fierce snarls and high-pitched screams around a carcass establish dominance.

WHAT'S IN A NAME?

How did the Tasmanian devil get such an odd name? Combine their eerie growls as they search for food with their harsh screeching and spine-chilling screams when they feed on a carcass, and it's not hard to see why European settlers to Australia named these animals devils.

TIME TO GO

After four months, the babies emerge from the mother's pouch. They either ride on their mother's back or are dragged along underneath her. When they are about six months old, the young are weaned and on their own.

OH, SURE!

The famous gape, or yawn, of the Tasmanian devil looks threatening, but it more likely expresses fear and uncertainty rather than aggression.

THE FIRST YEAR'S THE HARDEST

If a devil can survive the first year, its life span in the wild is about seven to eight years. Other threats come from domestic dogs, attack by adult devils, being hit by cars, loss of habitat, and disease.

WHERE IN THE WORLD ARE TASMANIAN DEVILS?

RANGE: the island of Tasmania

HABITAT: forests, woodlands, and agricultural areas (mostly coastal scrub and eucalyptus forests)

Bat

Black Flying Fox

BATS GREAT AND SMALL

Mega bats are medium- to large-sized bats. Many eat fruit, pollen, or nectar; some eat small land animals, and some eat fish. They have big eyes and excellent eyesight.

Micro bats are small bats that eat insects. They detect sound waves to navigate and identify the flying insects they eat. Included in this group is the smallest bat, the Kitti's hog-nosed bat.

BATS ARE MYTH-UNDERSTOOD

Bats roost upside down, usually in large social groups, in caves, trees, and man-made structures. Some bats migrate to warmer climates during the winter, while others hibernate.

NO VAMPIRE HERE

Only three species of bats, found from Mexico to South America, eat the blood of mammals or birds, often domestic animals like cows. These bats bite their victim then lick up the blood. They don't suck blood. The bite is more annoying than dangerous.

Bat Gardeners
Bats pollinate trees, flowers, and cacti. They also spread seeds so plants grow in new areas.

Indian Flying Fox

Spotted Bat

GONE FISHIN'

A few species of bats eat fish, lizards, frogs, birds, rodents, and even other bats. Fishing bats fly over water, bounce sound off the water to hear the fish, grab it with their sharp claws, and then stick it into their mouths.

INSECT CONTROL

About 70 percent of all bats eat flies, mosquitoes, beetles, and cockroaches. Millions of bats live together and each can eat half its weight in insects every night. A colony of bats in Texas eats 500,000 pounds of mosquitoes every night.

BAT WINGS

Bat wings contain four bones with a thin membrane spread across these bones. The membrane is connected to the bat's back and legs, like the fabric and ribs of an umbrella.

Got Milk?
All bats live on milk from birth up to six months of age.

FLYING PUPPIES

Bat babies are called pups. Mothers teach their pups how to fly and find food. A mother bat can locate her pup by its scent and sound out of millions in a roost.

Greater Mastiff Bat

WHERE IN THE WORLD ARE BATS?

RANGE: worldwide, except for extreme Arctic and desert regions

HABITAT: varied; most in tropical forests

HOW SWEET IT IS

Bats that drink nectar have long snouts and tongues. They lap up nectar as they hover over the blossoms. Their hair catches pollen and carries it from flower to flower.

Fruit Salad
Some bats eat fruit. They find their dinner by the smell of ripening fruit.

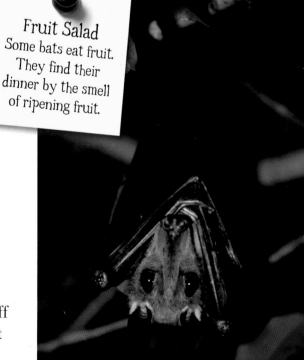
Hammer-headed Fruit Bat

I HEAR DINNER

Micro bats make high-pitched sounds that bounce off objects and return to the bat as echoes. Bats in flight can hear the difference between a tree, your head, and a tasty grasshopper. Bats see in black, white, and shades of gray. Most see better at night than day.

Otters

OTTER STUFF

LARGEST: giant otter, to 7.8 feet
SMALLEST: Asian small-clawed otter, to 3 feet
HEAVIEST: male sea otter, to 95 pounds
LIGHTEST: Asian small-clawed otter, to 11 pounds
LIFE SPAN: 15 to 20 years
NUMBER OF YOUNG AT BIRTH: 1 to 5, usually 2
SIZE AT BIRTH: smaller species, 4.5 ounces; sea otters, to 5 pounds
CONSERVATION STATUS: 4 species, including the sea otter, endangered; 3 otter species vulnerable

Spot-necked Otter

What Did You Say?
Otters make lots of sounds, from whistles, growls, and screams to barks, chirps, and coos.

CHAMPION SWIMMERS

An otter is made for swimming. Its tail is long and slightly flattened and moves sideways to propel it through the water, and almost all otters have webbed feet. When swimming underwater, otters close their ears and noses; their heart rate slows to use less oxygen. They can stay submerged for about five minutes.

Sea Otter (Superstock)

FUR COAT

Sea otters rely on warm air trapped in their fur to keep them warm. They have the densest fur of any mammal: about 100,000 hairs in a space about the size of a postage stamp. A dense undercoat traps air and a topcoat of long hairs keeps the undercoat dry. If their fur becomes matted with oil, otters can freeze.

North American River Otters

Sea Otter Eating (Superstock)

WHAT'S FOR BREAKFAST, LUNCH, AND DINNER?

Sea otters eat mostly sea urchins, abalone, crabs, mussels, and clams, which they crack open against rocks they hold on their stomachs. River otters eat fish, frogs, crayfish, crabs, and mollusks. River otters digest their food very fast, so they eat several times a day. Otters have long, sensitive whiskers that help them find prey, even in murky water.

What's for Dinner? Sea otters eat 20 to 25 percent of their body weight EVERY DAY.

SEA PUPPIES

Sea otter pups are born with their eyes open, and because of their buoyant fur, they can float, even though they can't swim. Pups ride on their mother's stomach for the first two months. Then they swim and dive on their own.

Sea Otter Mother and Pup (Minden)

RIVER PUPPIES

River otter pups are born in a den. They are helpless and don't open their eyes for the first month. They learn to swim at two months, and stay with their mother until they are about one year old.

WHERE IN THE WORLD ARE OTTERS?

RANGE: Africa, Asia, and parts of North, Central, and South America

HABITAT: rivers, lakes, marshes, Pacific Ocean and its coastline

European River Otter

Baby European River Otter

LET'S PARTY!

Otters are intelligent, curious, and usually busy hunting, investigating, or playing with something. They like to throw and bounce things, wrestle, twirl, and chase their tails. They play games of tag and chase each other, both in the water and on the ground. River otters slide down mud banks.

Sea Lion

California Sea Lion

SWIM, SEA LION, SWIM

Sea lions can swim up to 25 miles per hour for short bursts. This helps them escape from their enemies, killer whales and sharks.

I'm Not Thirsty!
Sea lions don't need to drink water. They get all the water they need from the food they eat.

California Sea Lion

WHAT'S THE DIFFERENCE?

How do you tell a sea lion from a seal? Both are marine mammals. Both have flippers at the end of their limbs. Both have a thick layer of blubber to keep them warm. Both eat lots of fish. So what's the difference? Their ears—if you see a small ear flap on each side of its head, you are looking at a sea lion. Seals just have a tiny opening for their ears. Sea lions also rotate their hind flippers forward to help them scoot along on land. Seals cannot do this, and must wriggle, hunch, roll, or slide.

DIVE, SEA LION, DIVE!

A sea lion dives up to 600 feet deep in search of fish and squid. Their nostrils automatically close when they dive and a sea lion can remain underwater for up to 40 minutes at a time.

WHERE IN THE WORLD ARE SEA LIONS?

RANGE: coastlines along both sides of the Pacific Ocean

HABITAT: oceans and rocky shorelines

COLONIES AND ROOKERIES

Sea lion families can number up to 15 cows and their young. A large group of sea lions gathered together on land or floating ice is called a colony. During the birthing season these areas are known as rookeries.

Adult Galápagos Sea Lions and Pup

Galápagos Sea Lion Pup

THESE LIONS ROAR

Sea lions bark, honk, trumpet, and roar. During breeding season, bulls bark loudly and continuously to establish or defend their territories. A pup can pick out its mother from among hundreds by the sound she makes.

Never Shipwrecked
A group of sea lions in the water is called a raft.

WHAT'S UP, PUP?

Sea lion pups are born on land in a gathering called a rookery. The males defend their territory on land while the females take care of the pups. Pups are born with their eyes open and their tummies ready for mother's rich milk. The milk is high in fat, and this helps the pup grow blubber to keep warm. At just a few weeks of age, sea lion pups are ready for their first swimming and fishing lessons.

Galápagos Sea Lions

LIONS ALL

Steller sea lions are the largest of the sea lions. They have thick, hairy necks that look like a lion's mane.

WHAT'S FOR DINNER?

Sea lions eat fish, squid, crabs, and clams. Most of the food is swallowed whole. The sea lion will toss the fish or squid up and around until it can slide headfirst down its mouth. They have flat back teeth and crunch the hard shells of clams before swallowing.

DO YOU FEEL DINNER YET?

Sea lions find their way around the dark ocean with the help of sensitive whiskers. Each long whisker, called a vibrissa, is loosely attached to the sea lion's upper lip. Like a straw in a soda bottle, each whisker rotates with the underwater currents, and the sea lion "feels" food swimming near.

California Sea Lion

Whales

WHALE STUFF

LONGEST: blue whale, 70 feet
SHORTEST: Hector's beaked whale, 4.5 feet
HEAVIEST: blue whale, 126,000 pounds (63 tons)
LIGHTEST: Hector's beaked whale, 105 pounds
LIFE SPAN: to 100 years
NUMBER OF YOUNG AT BIRTH: 1
SIZE AT BIRTH: 1/4 to 1/3 the length of the mother
CONSERVATION STATUS: 11 species endangered, including the blue whale, sperm whale, and humpback whale

Beluga Whale (Superstock)

I HEAR YOU

Toothed whales make sounds that travel underwater, bounce off an object, and then return to the whales as echoes. This echolocation allows the whale to find food or avoid predators, even in dark or murky water. The sounds do not come from the whales' throats. The sounds are made from air vibrating through the whales' nasal passages deep inside their heads.

BALEEN WHALES

There are 13 species of baleen whales, including the gray whale, blue whale, and humpback whale. Baleen whales have a double blowhole on top of the head. They gulp huge amounts of seawater, then strain the water to catch the zooplankton and krill. Gray whales suck up mud from the ocean floor and strain out the small worms and crustaceans that live there. No one knows whether or not baleen whales use echolocation.

Gray Whale Calf (Superstock)

Beluga Whale (Superstock)

WHAT IN THE WORLD IS BALEEN?

Baleen is made up of tough, flexible strands of keratin that hang down from the top of the whale's enormous mouth.

WHERE IN THE WORLD ARE WHALES?

RANGE: worldwide

HABITAT: oceans and seas of the world, some lakes and rivers

Fluke of a Humpback Whale (Superstock)

A WHALE OR A BIG FISH?

Whale tails are perpendicular to their bodies. Fish tails are flat-sided. Whales move their tails in an up-and-down motion. Fish tails move from side to side.

Teeth or Gums?
Whales are divided into two groups: toothed and baleen.

Humpback Whale (Minden)

GOING DOWN

Whales dive on a full breath of air. Their bodies send the oxygen to vital organs such as their brains, hearts, and lungs. Their heart rate slows. Sperm whales can dive more than one mile deep and stay for more than one hour.

White Sperm Whale (Minden)

MAMMALS OF THE SEA

Whales all have flippers, smooth skin, and flat tails (called flukes) that propel them through the water. They give birth and nurse their young in the water and live their entire lives there. They have excellent vision, large brains, and exhibit great intelligence.

WOW!
The blue whale is the largest mammal to have ever lived on earth.

TOOTHED WHALES

There are 69 species of toothed whales. These include sperm whales, beluga whales, narwhals, bottlenose dolphins, and killer whales. Toothed whales have one blowhole on top of the head and use echolocation to find food. These whales eat fish, octopus, squid, and crustaceans like shrimp.

WHALE SONGS

Whales make lots of different kinds of sounds, including trills, whistles, moans, and squeals. Single male humpback whales sing their whale songs during the winter mating season.

GOING SOUTH FOR THE WINTER

Gray whales make the longest migration of any whale. They travel from Alaska to the coast of Mexico. This is a round-trip journey of more than 12,000 miles.

BODIES MADE FOR SWIMMING

Dolphins have smooth skin, flippers, and dorsal fins. They have long, slender snouts and streamlined bodies.

BEDTIME

When dolphins sleep, they float about ten inches below the surface of the water. Every now and then their flukes move slightly and push them up to the surface to breathe.

Bottlenose Dolphin (Superstock)

Spotted Dolphin (Superstock)

STAYING AFLOAT

Dolphins are buoyant because of their bone and body structure and their ability to hold oxygen in their bodies.

WHERE IN THE WORLD ARE DOLPHINS?

RANGE: all the world's oceans

HABITAT: mainly coastal; some spend their lives at sea

Spinner Dolphin (Superstock)

SEEING STARS

The three best-known dolphins—white-sided dolphins, bottlenose dolphins, and spinner dolphins—can be seen in marine mammal demonstrations, on television shows, and in movies.

THE NOSE

The single blowhole on top of their heads has a flap that opens to reveal a pair of nostrils, which they use for breathing when they surface.

Bottlenose Dolphin (Superstock)

IT'S ALL RELATIVE

You might not realize that dolphins are closely related to whales. The scientific order, called Cetacea, includes dolphins, whales, and porpoises. The dolphin family has 36 species in all. It can get confusing at times, because some members of the dolphin family have the word "whale" in their common name. In fact, the largest dolphin is the killer whale! Depending on the species, dolphins range in color from white, pearl, and pink to darker shades of brown, gray, blue, and black.

Bottlenose Dolphin (Superstock)

What Big Teeth You Have!
Dolphins have about 100 cone-shaped, sharp pointed teeth that help to hold prey.

Bottlenose Dolphin (Superstock)

THE EYES HAVE IT

A dolphin has one eye on each side of its head, and each eye moves independently of the other. Dolphins can see ahead, to the side, and even behind them. They can also see very well both underwater and in the air. Their vision out of the water is about as good as a cat's or a dog's. Dolphins that live in rivers have much less well-developed vision.

Killer Whale (Superstock)

Water, Water Everywhere and Not a Drop to Drink
Dolphins don't drink sea water. They get the water they need from the bodies of the fish they eat.

A WHALE OF A TIME

Dolphins' natural abilities to swim fast and leap clear of the water are what make them such entertaining performers. They are the most agile and speedy of all marine mammals. They are known to travel with ships, leaping in front of the bow and swimming in the wake.

Bottlenose Dolphins (Superstock)

Bottlenose Dolphins (Superstock)

CLICKS AND WHISTLES

Dolphins use clicking sounds for echolocation, and many use whistles to communicate with other members of their pod. In addition to clicks and whistles, researchers have described dolphin sounds as screams, calls, moans, trills, grunts, squeaks, and even a "creaky door" sound. Bottlenose dolphin researchers think that slow clicks and high-pitched whistles are signs of contentment, whereas harsh, low squawks express annoyance.

DO YOU HEAR WHAT I HEAR?

Dolphins may have the best hearing of all animals. Their ear holes are only about the size of a crayon point, but they receive sound vibrations through their jawbones and heads. The vibrations then pass to the tiny bones of their inner ear.

If You Need Me, Just Whistle! Every dolphin has its own distinct whistle to communicate with others in its pod.

ECHO-CO-CO-CO

Dolphins make sounds that travel underwater, bounce off something, and then return to the dolphins as echoes. This sophisticated echolocation allows dolphins to find food or avoid predators, even in dark or murky water. Dolphins that live in rivers have excellent echolocation for fishing in muddy waters.

Spotted Dolphins (Superstock)

Pacific White-sided Dolphin (Minden)

Bottlenose Dolphin (Superstock)

WHAT'S FOR DINNER?

Most dolphins eat fish, octopus, squid, and shrimp. Killer whales' diet include seals, smaller whales, penguins, birds, and even small walruses. Dolphins herd schools of fish, just like sheepdogs herd sheep, using their clicking sounds. Bottlenose dolphins even rush up onto mud banks to catch fish stranded there.

SCHOOL'S NEVER OUT!

Dolphins live and play in schools of five to hundreds of animals. Some can swim and roll in formation, just like synchronized swimmers. Pods of dolphins will attack an intruder as a group and will kill large sharks by ramming them as a group.

Bottlenose Dolphins (Minden)

Mother Spotted Dolphin and Calf (Superstock)

EMERGENCY CARE

If a dolphin is sick or hurt, the others in the pod help. They also help female dolphins when they give birth. Dolphins in the pod take turns pushing the hurt or young dolphin to the surface so it can breathe.

Churchill, Manitoba Canada

Habitats

WHAT IN THE WORLD ARE HABITATS?

- are natural environments
- provide homes for animals
- provide for specific types of plants

San Clemente Island

Seal Rock

Costa Rica
Rainforest

Borrego Springs

WHAT ARE THE NAMES OF SOME HABITATS?

Deserts	Wetlands
Islands	Savannas
Oceans	Scrublands
Prairies	Taigas
Steppes	Temperate Forests
Rivers	Tropical Rain Forests
Lakes	Tundras

Deserts

Dunes Near Yuma

BRRR, I'M FREEZING IN THIS DESERT!
Temperatures can be as high as 120°F in some deserts. Because there is no cloud cover to keep warmth in, deserts get very cold at night, with temperatures as low as -4°F. Deserts can be windy with violent sand storms.

SO, WHAT'S SO DIFFERENT ABOUT A DESERT?

Deserts are hot, dry places made up mostly of sand, rock, and mountains. Deserts are areas where more water evaporates in the air than falls to the ground as rain. Now that's dry!

WHERE IN THE WORLD ARE DESERTS?

the Namib and Kalahari deserts in Africa, the Arabian desert, the Great Victoria desert in Australia, and the Mojave and Sonora deserts in the United States

California High Desert

GET OUT OF THE HEAT!

Animals that live in the desert live underground or hide in burrows during the hottest part of the day. Some animals get the moisture they need from their food, so they don't need to drink much water. Other animals live at the edge of deserts, where there are more plants and shelter.

NOT MUCH GREEN

Desert plants have thin, tough leaves or succulent stems, like cactus, to store water. Some plants are dormant during dry times, and only come to life when it rains.

Turks and Caicos

Islands

SO, WHAT'S SO DIFFERENT ABOUT AN ISLAND?

All island ecosystems are isolated from the mainland, and they create special environments. Animals and plants may be very different from any others. Some animals are only found on islands.

DON'T ROCK THE ISLAND

Island ecosystems are fragile and easily disturbed by animals that have been brought from outside. The habitat is also disturbed by humans. This is because the island's land is small and the resources are limited.

STRANGE ANIMALS

The kiwi bird is found only on the island of New Zealand. The Galápagos tortoise lives only in the Galápagos Islands.

Galápagos Island

NOWHERE TO GO

If the habitat of the animals is destroyed, or if what they eat disappears, island animals can quickly become endangered. On an island, there is nowhere else for the animals to go.

WHERE IN THE WORLD ARE ISLANDS?

Almost every part of the world. Habitats include rain forest, temperate forest, tundra, and desert.

SO, WHAT'S SO DIFFERENT ABOUT AN OCEAN?

An ocean is not just one type of habitat. Where an ocean is in the world and how deep it is affects the light, pressure, temperature, and nutrients in the ocean. That determines what can live there.

Oceans & Coastlines

Seal Rock, California

OCEAN-DESERT?

Most of the ocean is actually like a desert, with few resources for animals and plants to live on. In the open ocean there are underwater vents or volcanoes that release minerals and gases. These minerals and gases support life.

WHERE IN THE WORLD ARE OCEANS?

All over the world. The earth has five oceans, and 70 percent of the earth is under the waters of the oceans.

So, What's So Different About a Coastline?

The land that surrounds the oceans, the coastlines, release nutrients from the land into the sea. This helps provide a habitat for many animals and plants. Coastlines are usually divided into rocky, sandy, or muddy types. Each has its own ecosystem.

On the Move and Having It All

Birds, fish, turtles, and marine mammals can travel and take advantage of the best temperatures, light, and food. The gray whales, the dolphins, and the leatherback sea turtle, for example, travel long distances.

Here Today, Gone Tomorrow

Coastlines are only about eight percent of the earth's land. Here live seabirds, clams, crabs, starfish, anemones, fish, kelp, and marine mammals. The coastline can be a hard place to live when it is battered by waves and soaked in salty seaspray; and storms and the tides constantly erode the coastline.

Prairies & Steppes

Prairie in Fort Macleod. Alberta, Canada (Superstock)

So, What's So Different about Prairies & Steppes?

Prairies and steppes are grasslands habitats that are hot in the summer and cold in the winter.

WHAT'S WAVING ON THE PRAIRIE?

Grasses of many different types grow on prairies and steppes, and these have varying degrees of drought tolerance. Some don't tolerate dryness at all and die. Others have strong roots to store nutrients and flexible stems so as not to snap in the strong winds.

WHERE DID EVERYBODY GO?

A prairie may look desolate, but it is actually a fertile and diverse habitat that can be home to 80 different mammal species and more than 300 species of birds.

The Great Dust Bowl
Grasses can disappear if a prairie is overgrazed or farmed intensively. Then the topsoil can erode and blow away.

THE FISHING'S GOOD

Creeks and streams run through these grassy prairies and trees line their banks. Prairies also have rock outcroppings that provide shelter for animals.

WHERE IN THE WORLD ARE PRAIRIES AND STEPPES?

Prairies: North and South America

Steppes: Asia and Australia

Rivers, Lakes & Wetlands

Tijuana Estuary

LAKES & RIVERS
Every lake and river has its own types of plants
and animals, depending on how fast the water
moves and is replaced, the nature of the rocks and
soil, and the chemical make-up of the water itself.

WETLANDS
Wetlands are constantly changing, based on the seasons,
water levels, tides, and migrations of birds and mammals.

HOME, WET HOME
Wetlands are best known as a home
for hundreds of bird species, from
herons and storks to eagles,
kingfishers, and ibises.

Tijuana Estuary

So, What's So Different about a Wetland?

Wetlands may have areas of permanent standing water, although that may change with rainy and dry seasons. Wetlands may also be areas of damp, muddy, waterlogged soil. These include marshes, swamps, bogs, and lagoons.

WHERE IN THE WORLD ARE RIVERS, LAKES & WETLANDS?

everywhere, from polar regions to the tropics

WATER SUPPORTS LIFE

Rivers and lakes are freshwater habitats that support many forms of life, from algae and plankton to insects and fish to larger animals. The food chain and the interdependence of the plants and animals in these habitats can be disrupted by pollution, pesticides, and erosion.

Savannas

Kalahari Scene, Kgalagadi Transfrontier Park, South Africa (Superstock)

SO, WHAT'S SO DIFFERENT ABOUT A SAVANNA?

Savannas are made up of large expanses of grasses, often one or two species that create a continuous carpet, interrupted by scattered shrubs and trees.

WHAT MAKES A SAVANNA?

A savanna is born when there is not enough rain to support a tropical rain forest, but there is enough to keep the land from becoming a desert.

WHO ON EARTH LIVES ON THE SAVANNA?

The savanna is home to large herds of grazing animals and the predators that follow them, such as giraffes, gazelles, and lions.

RUN! FIRE!

Fire has an important role in the savanna. It burns out old grass growth and new tree saplings, making way for the new grasses that animals like gazelles depend upon.

WHERE IN THE WORLD ARE SAVANNAS?

the tropical areas throughout the world: east African plains, South American pampas, and the open woodlands of northern Australia

TO EVERYTHING THERE IS A SEASON

There is usually a dry season and a rainy season in the savanna, with strong, hot winds in the dry season and enough rain in the wet season to flood low-lying areas.

DON'T TIP THE SAVANNA

A savanna is a carefully balanced ecosystem that can easily be disturbed by changes in climate, an imbalance in the number and type of animal species, and human influences such as farming and cattle herding.

Scrublands

Taos, New Mexico (Superstock)

STAY AWAY!
Many plants in scrublands have thorns and strong-smelling oils to protect themselves from hungry herbivores.

FROM LITTLE ACORNS GROW LITTLE SCRUB TREES
Some trees grow here, such as oaks, pines, and cypress, but they don't get very large. An exception is in the scrubland forest of Australia, where the eucalyptus trees can be quite tall. Most of the plants in these habitats are scrub plants.

YOU'VE GOTTA BE TOUGH TO MAKE IT!

In scrublands, some plants may lie dormant during the summer. They bud and bloom in the autumn and grow when the rainfall comes in winter. In summer, the plants drop their leaves; have tough, leathery leaves that retain water; or die back to their roots to survive.

WHERE IN THE WORLD ARE SCRUBLANDS?

the chaparral in California, mallee in Australia, fynbos in South Africa, and mattoral in Chile

Temperate Forests & Taigas

Lac Fortune, Gatineau Park, Quebec, Canada (Superstock)

SO, WHAT'S SO DIFFERENT ABOUT A TEMPERATE FOREST?

A temperate forest is one in which there is enough rainfall to allow trees, shrubs, flowers, ferns, and mosses to flourish, while also following the rhythm of the seasons: sun and warm temperatures in the summer, and snow and cold temperatures in the winter.

THE DIVERSITY OF LIFE

The interactions between the trees, shrubs, and undergrowth of temperate forests and taiga are complex and dynamic, as they respond to changes in soil, water, seasons, and climate. This creates a diverse ecosystem containing several types of woodland communities. The rich soil, leaf litter, fallen trees, and living forest provide homes and food sources for a wide variety of animal and insect species.

SO, WHAT'S SO DIFFERENT ABOUT A TAIGA?

Taiga is also a type of forest habitat. It is sometimes called a boreal forest, but it is much colder and can remain under ice and snow for more than six months of the year. The forest trees here are mostly conifers and evergreens, like spruce, pine, fir, and larch.

How Old Is Old?
Trees in "old growth" forests can be 120 years old or more. They survived storms and drought and fires to reach that age.

THEN AND NOW
Very few of the earth's temperate forests have remained untouched by humans, and vast areas that used to be covered by ancient, "old growth" forests are now occupied by cities and farmland.

WHERE IN THE WORLD ARE TEMPERATE FORESTS & TAIGAS?

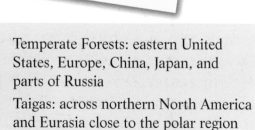

Temperate Forests: eastern United States, Europe, China, Japan, and parts of Russia

Taigas: across northern North America and Eurasia close to the polar region

Tropical Rain Forests

Costa Rican Rain Forest

TEEMING WITH TREASURES

Tropical rain forests are some of the world's most important natural resources, filled with biological treasures. A typical four-square-mile section can contain over 1,500 species of flowering plants, 750 species of trees, 125 species of birds, 100 species of reptiles, 60 species of amphibians, and 150 species of butterflies. Many species have not even been discovered by scientists yet.

SO, WHAT'S SO DIFFERENT ABOUT A TROPICAL RAIN FOREST?

A tropical rain forest gets more than 60 inches of rain per year, although some regularly get more than 200 inches! For comparison, San Diego gets around nine inches of rain per year.

UP IN SMOKE!

Tropical rain forests need our help. Too much of them has been destroyed by burning, logging, ranching, and poor farming practices. If people work together, we can find many ways to use the rain forest without destroying it.

New Guinea Rain Forest

So, Who Lives in
a Rain Forest?
The rain forests of the world are
home to many unusual plants
and fascinating animals like the
Javan rhinoceros hornbill.

WHERE IN THE WORLD ARE TROPICAL RAIN FORESTS?

Look on a globe and find the
equator. Tropical rain forests form a
green band around the equator
between the two imaginary lines of
the tropics of Cancer and Capricorn.

FOOD FOR THOUGHT

Every day, people eat foods that started
out in the rain forest. Each time you
eat bananas, oranges, grapefruit,
chocolate, chicken or chicken eggs,
papayas, pineapples, rice, corn,
potatoes, tomatoes, and peanuts, you
are eating gifts from the rain forest.

Tundras

Churchill, Manitoba, Canada

So, What's So Different about a Tundra?

The tundra has temperatures as low as -76°F in the winter with almost no sunlight and temperatures as high as 77°F in the short summer season. Even with the warm summer, however, the lower levels of soil remain frozen all year, and this is known as permafrost.

Some Like It Cold!

A surprising variety of plants manage to live on the tundra by growing and producing seeds quickly to take advantage of the summer sun and warmth, then dying back or hardening up against the winter cold. These plants tend to grow shallow roots over a wide area to avoid the permafrost, and they tend to grow low to the ground—even the few trees like the dwarf willow—to avoid the bitter and dehydrating tundra wind.

Churchill, Manitoba Canada

IT'S A NICE PLACE TO VISIT, BUT . . .

Many animals found on the tundra are migratory species, moving in to eat the plants in the summer, but leaving again before the hard winter. Some remain all year, though, like the polar bear, the musk ox, and the snowy owl.

WHERE IN THE WORLD ARE TUNDRAS?

in the Arctic, beyond the permanent ice pack that surrounds the North Pole

Animal Group Names

Some animal groups have some pretty amazing names. Did you know that a group of frogs is called an "army"? Or that a group of porcupines is called a "prickle" of porcupines? Take a look at other group names and see which ones you think are funny. Gulp! What do you call it when cormorants congregate?

alligators: congregation
antelope: herd
ants: nest, army, colony, swarm
apes: troop, shrewdness
asses: pace, herd, drove
baboons: troop
badgers: cete
bears: sloth, sleuth
beavers: family, colony
bees: grist, swarm, nest, hive
boars: sounder, singular
buffalo: herd, troop, gang, obstinancy
butterflies: flutter
buzzards: wake
camels: train, caravan, flock
caribou: herd
cats: clowder, cluster, glaring, pounce

caterpillars: army
cattle: drove, herd
chickens: brood, peep
cockroaches: intrusion
cormorants: gulp
cows: kine
crocodiles: bask, float
crows: murder
deer: herd
dogs: pack
doves: arc, dule, flight, pitying
ducks: paddling, flock, raft
eagles: aerie, convocation
eels: bed, swarm
elephants: herd, memory
elks: gang, herd
emus: mob

ferrets: business
finches: charm
fish: school, shoal, haul, catch
flamingos: stand, flamboyance
flies: swarm, cloud, business
foxes: leash, skulk, troop
frogs: army
geese: gaggle, skein
giraffes: herd, corps, tower
gnats: swarm, cloud, horde
goats: flock, herd, tribe, trip
goldfish: troubling
gorillas: band, troop
grasshoppers: cloud
gulls: colony
hares: down, husk
hawks: boil, cast, kettle
herons: sedge, siege
hippopotamuses: bloat
horses: herd, band, string, team, stable
hounds: mute, brace, pack
hyenas: cackle
jays: band, party, scold
jellyfish: smack, brood
kangaroos: mob, herd, troop
larks: exaltation
leopards: leap
lions: pride
lizards: lounge
mice: nest
moles: labor
monkeys: barrel (really!)
moose: herd
mules: barren, span
otters: romp
oxen: team, yoke, drove
owls: parliament
oysters: bed
parrots: company, pandemonium
peacocks: ostentation, pride
pelicans: pod
penguins: rookery, colony
pheasants: bouquet, nye
pigs: drift, drove, sounder

porcupines: prickle
porpoises: school, crowd, shoal
prairie dogs: coterie
quail: bevy, covey
rabbits: nest, warren
raccoons: gaze
rattlesnakes: rhumba
ravens: unkindness
rhinoceroses: crash
sardines: family
seabirds: wreck
seals: pod, rookery
sharks: school, shoal
sheep: flock, pack, hurtle
snakes: bed, knot, den, pit
sparrows: host
spiders: clutter
squirrels: dray, scurry
starlings: chattering, murmuration
storks: mustering
swallows: flight
swans: bevy, herd, bank, wedge, flight
swine: sounder, drift, herd
tigers: ambush, streak
toads: nest, knot
trout: hover
turkeys: rafter
turtles: bale, dole
walruses: pod, herd
weasels: pack, colony
whales: school, pod, mob, gam
wolves: pack, rout
wombats: wisdom
woodpeckers: descent
zebras: herd, zeal

Glossary

A

abalone: An edible mollusk that lives in the warm ocean and has an ear-shaped shell.

abdomen: Part of the body that contains the digestive tract. In insects, the back area, behind the thorax.

algae: Simple plants that have chlorophyll but no stems, roots, nor leaves; seaweed.

alpha: The most powerful animal in a group.

ambush: A surprise attack.

Antarctica: A continent that surrounds the South Pole.

antennae: A pair of long, thin appendages that are sensitive to touch on some insects, crustaceans, and arthropods.

aquatic: Growing or living in the water.

arachnid: A class of arthropods that includes spiders, ticks, and scorpions.

Arctic: The area around the North Pole.

arthropods: Invertebrate animals with an exoskeleton, segmented body, and jointed legs, such as spiders, insects, and crustaceans.

B

barbule: A tiny branch that sprouts from the barb of a feather.

backbone: The spine of an animal.

baleen: The elastic, horny material forming fringed plates that hang from the upper jaw of baleen whales used for straining plankton and krill from the water.

barb: A branch growing from the shaft of a feather.

beak: The horny projecting jaw of a bird.

beeswax: The secretion of bees that forms the honeycomb.

bill: A bird's flat beak.

blubber: The thick layer of fat of sea mammals, especially sea lions and whales.

borer: A worm, insect, or larva that bores into wood or plants.

buck: The male of some animals, including deer, antelope, and rabbits.

bull: The male of some animals, including elephants and alligators.

burrow: A hole or tunnel dug by an animal.

C

caiman: An animal similar to an alligator that is found in Central and South America.

carapace: The upper portion of the shell of a turtle.

carcass: The dead body of an animal.

carnivore: An animal that eats meat.

carotenoid: Red, yellow, or orange pigments that give color to plants.

carrion: Decaying flesh of a dead animal.

caterpillar: The larva of a butterfly or moth.

cephalothorax: The joined head and thorax of spiders and arthropods.

chick: A newly hatched bird.

chitin: A material that forms the exoskeleton of arthropods.

chrysalis: A pupa, such as a moth or butterfly, enclosed in a firm case or cocoon.

claw: A curved, pointed, horny nail on the toes of birds, lizards, and some mammals.

colony: A community of animals living together.

communication: The exchange of news, wants, or needs.

compound eye: An eye that contains several small vision segments.

coniferous: Trees that bear cones and have evergreen, needle-like leaves.

constrict: Applying pressure to reduce air supply.

cow: The fully grown female of some animals, including elephants and whales.

crevice: A thin, narrow opening in a rock.

crop: A pouch in a bird's gullet or esophagus where food is stored and prepared for digestion.

crop milk: Nourishing liquid made by some birds to feed their chicks.

crustacean: A group of arthropods that includes shrimp, crabs, and lobsters.

cuticle: A waxy, hard layer that covers and protects an invertebrate.

D

deciduous: A tree or shrub that sheds its leaves every winter.

dentine: Hard, bony tissue under the enamel that makes up teeth or tusks.

desert: A dry land with little vegetation.

digestion: The process of breaking down food so the body can use it.

down: The soft, fine, fluffy first feathers on a chick.

drone: A male bee whose only job is to fertilize the queen.

dung: Animals' solid bodily waste.

E

eaglet: A young eagle.

echolocation: The location of objects using reflected sound (echoes).

ectothermic: An animal whose body temperature is regulated by outside sources of heat.

egg: An oval or round object laid by a female bird, reptile, fish, or invertebrate that contains developing offspring.

egg tooth: A tooth that the embryos of some birds and reptiles use to break their egg in hatching and which is later lost.

elytra: The wing cases on the back of the beetle.

endangered: At risk of extinction.

environment: The surroundings in which something lives or exists, including air, water, land, natural resources, plants, and animals.

eucalyptus: A variety of tall trees with aromatic leaves native to Australia.

exoskeleton: A hard outer structure that provides protection for some invertebrates, including crustaceans and insects.

extinct: An animal or plant that has no living members left on the earth.

F

feces: Animals' discharged waste matter.

fluke: The flat end of a whale's tail.

fossil: The remains of a prehistoric plant or animal that has been preserved in rock.

G

gharial: A large, fish-eating crocodile native to India.

gills: The organ in a fish that takes oxygen from water.

gizzard: The muscular, thick-walled part of a bird's stomach that grinds food.

graze: To feed on grass out in a field.

gut: The stomach.

H

habitat: The natural home of a plant or animal.

hatch: To emerge from an egg.

hatchling: A young animal recently emerged from an egg.

herbivore: An animal that eats only plants.

hibernate: To spend the winter asleep or in a slowed state.

hind leg: A leg at the back of the body.

hive: The home and workplace of bees.

honeycomb: A structure of six-sided cells in which bees store honey.

I

ibex: A wild goat found in Asia, Ethiopia, and Europe.

immune system: Part of the body that protects an animal from infection.

incisor: A flat, sharp tooth in the front of the mouth.

incubate: Keep eggs warm.

invertebrate: Animal with no backbone.

J

joey: A young kangaroo, wallaby, or koala.

K

keratin: Fibrous protein that makes up hair, feathers, claws, horns, and hooves.

knuckle walk: The ability of chimpanzees and gorillas to walk on the knuckles of their hands along with their feet.

krill: A small, shrimplike crustacean eaten by baleen whales.

L

larva: Immature form of an insect that looks nothing like the adult.

life span: Length of life.

M

mandible: The lower jawbone; also, the upper or lower part of a bird's beak.

mangrove: A tree or shrub that grows in muddy coastal swamps.

marsupial: A mammal whose offspring are born underdeveloped and must remain in the mother's pouch until developed.

marsupium: The pouch of a female marsupial in which she carries her underdeveloped baby.

mate: Bring together to produce offspring.

matriarch: A female who is head of a family group.

maturity: The time when an animal becomes an adult.

membrane: A pliable structure that covers an organism.

metamorphosis: The process of transforming an immature organism to a mature organism in two or more stages.

migrate: Move from one habitat to another, especially according to the seasons.

mollusk: An invertebrate that lives in an aquatic habitat, such as a snail, slug, or octopus.

molt: To shed old shells, feathers, or skin to make way for the new.

mucous: Producing, relating to, or covered with mucus.

N

nectar: A sugary fluid secreted by plants and collected by bees and hummingbirds.

nervous system: A network of cells and fibers that transmit impulses between parts of the body.

nest: A place where an animal or insect breeds or shelters.

nostrils: External openings of the nasal cavity.

nutrient: A substance that provides nourishment for growth or life.

nymph: An immature form of insect that does not change much in appearance as it grows.

O

omnivorous: An animal that eats both plants and animals.

opposable: A thumb or big toe on primates capable of moving toward and touching the other digits on the same hand or foot.

ossicones: The hair-covered horns of giraffes.

P

pachyderm: A very large mammal with thick skin, such as an elephant, rhinoceros, or hippopotamus.

pacing: A gait of four-legged animals in which they move both legs on the same side of the body at the same time.

papillae: Small rounded parts on the body.

parasite: An organism that lives off another organism.

pecking order: The order of status among animals.

perpendicular: A line at an angle of 90°.

pesticide: A substance used to kill insects that injure plants or other animals.

pigment: The natural coloring of plant or animal tissue.

plains: Large areas of flat land with few trees.

plankton: Small and microscopic organisms floating in the sea.

plastron: The underside of a tortoise's or turtle's shell.

pollen: A powdery substance, usually yellow, of microscopic grains discharged by the male part of the flower.

pollinate: To take pollen from one plant and deposit it into another flower.

pollution: The presence in the environment of a harmful substance.

pounce: To spring suddenly upon a prey.

prairie: A large open area of grassland.

predator: An animal that preys on other animals.

preen: When a bird straightens and cleans its feathers.

prehensile: Capable of grasping.

prehistoric: From the period before written history.

primate: A mammal with hands, handlike feet, and forward-facing eyes.

proboscis: A long, flexible snout or trunk, such as that of an elephant.

protein: Organic compound that is the essential part of body tissues, such as hair and muscles.

pupa: An insect in its immature form between the larva and chrysalis.

Q

queen bee: The only female in a beehive that can reproduce.

R

rain forest: A dense forest rich in diverse animals and plants, mainly found in tropical areas with heavy rainfall.

rectilinear progression: The straight-line movement of a snake.

regurgitate: To bring swallowed food up to the mouth.

reproduction: The production of offspring.

rodents: Gnawing mammals, such as mice, rats, hamsters, and squirrels.

rookery: A breeding colony of penguins, seals, or turtles.

roost: The act or place where birds gather at night to rest.

rosette: A marking that resembles a rose.

ruminant: A mammal that chews regurgitated food, or cud.

S

sap: Fluid that circulates in the vascular system of a plant.

savanna: A grassy plain with few trees in a tropical or subtropical region.

scrub land: Region covered with stunted forest growth.

scute: The horny or bony plate on the back of a tortoise's or turtle's shell, also the scales on the underside of a snake.

sea urchin: A marine animal that has a round shell covered in spines.

secretion: A substance discharged by a gland or organ for a particular purpose.

setae: Stiff, hairlike structures.

silverback: A mature gorilla with silver hair down its back that acts as the dominant gorilla in the troop.

simple eye: The small eye of an insect with only one lens.

siren: An eel-like amphibian.

skeleton: Internal or external framework of cartilage or bone.

skink: A smooth lizard with short or no limbs.

slug: A tough-skinned land mollusk with no shell that secrets a mucous.

species: A group of like organisms.

stalk: To approach something quietly so as not to be noticed.

stallion: An adult male horse or zebra.

steppes: Large unforested flatlands in Siberia and Europe.

subspecies: A group of like organisms within the species.

swamp: A lowland region where water collects.

T

tadpole: The larva of an amphibian that must live in the water.

tapetum: A reflective layer in the eyes of some mammals that cause them to shine in the dark.

terrain: The physical features of an area of land.

thorax: The part of an a animal between the neck and the abdomen.

toxic: A poisonous substance.

tundra: A vast, flat region in the Arctic in which the subsoil is permanently frozen.

tusk: A long, pointed tooth that protrudes from the closed mouths of elephants, walruses, and other mammals.

U

undercoat: The soft, downy fur underneath the longer outer coat of hair of a mammal.

urine: A yellowish, watery fluid stored in the bladder; serves to remove waste from the body.

urticating hairs: Hairs that can be thrown by some animals that can cause a stinging sensation.

V

venom: Poisonous fluid secreted by some snakes and animals.

vertebrae: Bones that form the backbone in animals.

vertebrate: Animal with a backbone.

vibrissae: Stiff hairs on the face of mammals that are sensitive to touch; whiskers.

vole: A burrowing, mouselike rodent.

vulnerable: Susceptible to harm.

vulture: A large bird of prey with no feathers on its head.

W

webbed feet: Feet of an animal characterized by toes connected by a membrane.

weevil: A small beetle whose larvae develop inside seeds or plants.

wetland: Land saturated by water, such as marshes and swamps.

winter sleep: A light hibernation.

woodland: Region with areas of land covered by forests.

Index